VOICELEADING JAZZGUITAR

Creative Voice Leading & Chord Substitution for Jazz Rhythm Guitar

JOSEPHALEXANDER

FUNDAMENTALCHANGES

Voice Leading Jazz Guitar

Creative Voice Leading & Chord Substitution for Jazz Rhythm Guitar

Published by **www.fundamental-changes.com**

ISBN: 978-1-78933-071-7

Copyright © 2019 Joseph Alexander

www.fundamental-changes.com

Twitter: @guitar_joseph

Over 10,000 fans on Facebook: **FundamentalChangesInGuitar**

Instagram: **FundamentalChanges**

For over 350 Free Guitar Lessons with Videos Check Out

www.fundamental-changes.com

The audio examples in this book are available for free download from:

www.fundamental-changes.com

Simply click the 'Download Audio' link at the top of the page.

Massive thanks to the wonderful Pete Sklaroff for recording the audio and his eternal patience and support in writing this book.

Cover Image Copyright © ShutterStock: Miguel Garcia Saaved

Contents

Introduction

This book examines the art of smooth, musical voice leading in jazz rhythm guitar. While it is intended to be a standalone guide to jazz rhythm guitar playing, unless you are familiar with many types of jazz guitar chord structures (such as drop 2 and drop 3 voicings), you might find this book quite challenging. I highly recommend working through this book in conjunction with my other book **Jazz Guitar Chord Mastery**.

The aim of this book is to get you thinking in terms of how intervals move fluidly on the guitar as chords change in a jazz tune. The idea is to move the fewest possible notes from your current chord to form a rich, interesting voicing for the next. The ultimate goal is to be able to play full jazz standards without having to jump around the fretboard, and so each note or *voice* moves as smoothly as possible.

In jazz, there are many possible *extensions and alterations* that can be used on any chord, and you will learn to instantly locate all the available musical choices for any chord and seamlessly incorporate them into your playing. Learning to incorporate extensions into your music can be a daunting task, and much advice is given about how to logically organise them into your practice.

This book also covers many useful *chord substitutions* with great focus on the concept of *secondary dominants*. By using substitutions, it is possible to create a rich, seamless tapestry of chord voicings that sound beautiful and effortless.

Chord substitutions are introduced naturally into your vocabulary and are used when musically appropriate. The most common substitutions are taught with explanations of why they work and when to use them.

Secondary dominant chords are a little complex, but they are given special attention with many examples of how to bring these creative devices into your jazz guitar comping.

Building from the concept of secondary dominants, we also explore the ideas behind tritone substitutions and some of their advanced applications. In doing so, we open up many voicing possibilities and some beautiful ways to navigate between otherwise 'standard' jazz chord changes.

Throughout this book, great care is taken to keep each concept musical, relevant and above all practical. Each example is based around one of two common jazz standards, and while for copyright reasons I can't name each tune, let's just call these standards *Bella by Barlight* and *Some of the Things You Are*.

The chord progressions for these songs are deconstructed and taught with great attention to detail. The emphasis throughout is to teach you the most important concepts of voice leading while developing your vision on the guitar and your musical ear. Soon you will begin to see the guitar neck in terms of intervals and possibilities, rather than being confined to the standard chord 'grips' that you probably use.

The one principle that will completely revolutionise the way you play jazz guitar is to learn to see the guitar neck purely in terms of *intervals*. While there is nothing wrong with seeing a B7 chord as:

Bb7

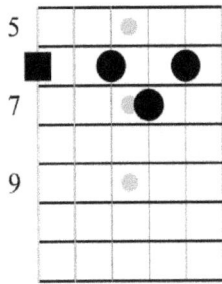

It is much more useful to see it like this:

Bb7

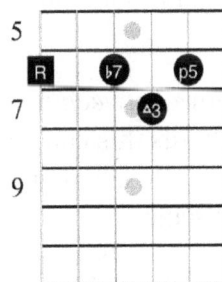

However, as you progress through this book you will learn to see it like this:

Bb7

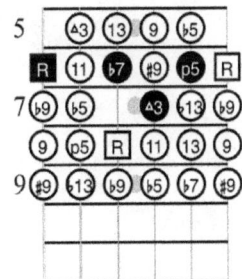

The thing to realise is that all of these extensions are available most of the time, and they are used naturally and frequently in jazz rhythm guitar.

We will cover extensions and alterations in later chapters, but for now you just need to know that one major outcome from studying this book is that you will start to 'see the matrix', and view the guitar neck as a palette of intervals or 'colours' with which to paint sounds.

The whole point of this book is to teach you to see the neck as a continuous, fluid succession of intervals that change with each chord. For example, the previous diagram views the neck from the point of view of a Bb7 chord. Everything changes if we view the neck around an Eb7 chord:

Eb7

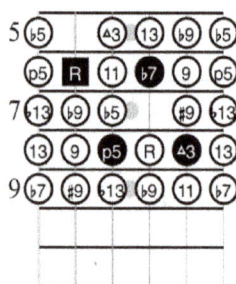

These diagrams may seem complex, but this level of vision does develop naturally with time, work and patience.

I don't want to scare you off, especially in the introduction, so just trust that this kind of insight is something that gradually grows while you're working on other things.

I mention all this now because an underpinning principle of harmony is that *you can often move between two seemingly unrelated chords by moving just one or two notes.* When playing 'normal' guitar chords this can be hard to see as you may move large distances, but when we study voice leading we can see how closely many chords are linked. The trick is to see which notes must move and which notes can remain the same.

The other important thing to understand is that root notes tend to be optional. Normally, another instrument will be taking care of the root, but even if they aren't, by using good voice leading the strength of the musical idea will normally be enough to allow the audience to hear and feel the harmony.

By removing the root, we free our fingers to reach beautiful extensions and keep the voice leading between chords as close as possible.

For example, instead of Fm7 to Bb7 played like this…

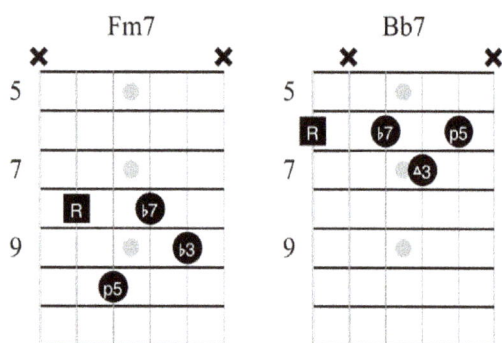

Fm7   Bb7

…we can learn to play voicings like the ones below by combining rootless chords with extensions while still retaining the harmonic function of each chord.

Fm9

```
      Fm9
  ✕         ✕
┌─┬─┬─┬─┐
5 │ │p5│ │
├─┼─┼─┼─┤
 ♭7 ♭3 │ │
7 │ │ ○ │
├─┼─┼─┼─┤
 ◻ │ 9 │
9 │ │ ○ │
```

Bb13

```
      Bb13
  ✕         ✕
┌─┬─┬─┬─┐
5 △3 │ 9 │
├─┼─┼─┼─┤
 ◻ │ ♭7 │
7 │ │ ○ │
├─┼─┼─┼─┤
 │ │ 13 │
9 │ │ ○ │
```

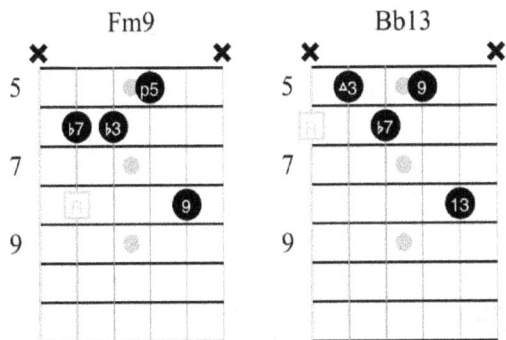

All the essential ingredients of each chord are included, but the voicings are richer and the voice leading is smoother as only one note moves between each chord.

This kind of vision and insight takes the right kind of practice, and this is exactly what this book sets out to teach you. The examples build chapter by chapter from simple first principles until you are set on your own path of musical discovery. This book teaches you a great deal, but the real fun begins when you take each concept and make it your own.

As with any book, I have had to assume certain things about your musical knowledge. It will help if you're familiar with chord construction and the concept of extensions. When it is relevant, I will refresh the basics in this book, but you will benefit from owning the books Guitar Chords in Context and Jazz Guitar Chord Mastery unless you already have a solid grounding in harmony.

The concepts in this book aren't just relevant for jazz guitar comping; they will deepen your insight into all areas of music and also greatly influence your jazz guitar soloing. Every chord idea is also a soloing idea: simply play the arpeggio instead of the chord voicing.

Have fun!

Joseph.

*The audio examples in this book are available for free download from **www.fundamental-changes.com** Simply click the 'Download Audio' link at the top of the page.*

Get the Audio

The audio files for this book are available to download for free from www.fundamental-changes.com. The link is in the top right-hand corner. Simply select this book title from the drop-down menu and follow the instructions to get the audio.

We recommend that you download the files directly to your computer, not to your tablet, and extract them there before adding them to your media library. You can then put them on your tablet, iPod or burn them to CD. On the download page there is a help PDF and we also provide technical support via the contact form.

For over 350 Free Lessons with Videos Check out:

www.fundamental-changes.com

Over 10,000 fans on Facebook: **FundamentalChangesInGuitar**

Instagram: **FundamentalChanges**

Chapter One: Simple Paths

To begin our journey into jazz guitar voice leading we need a workhorse set of chord changes that we can dissect to create real-world examples. I have chosen the jazz classic, Bella by Barlight as it contains some very interesting harmony, and it is a common tune called at jazz jams. The chord changes to Bella by Barlight are as follows:

To begin our exploration, we will focus on finding a path through the chords of the first four bars of the tune using simple voice leading and ignoring any possible alterations and extensions.

The chord sequence of the first four bars is:

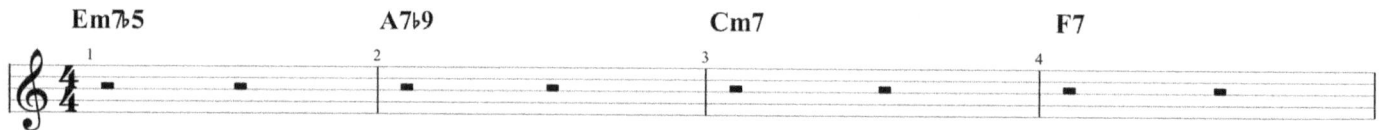

The object of the first exercise is to play through these chord changes while keeping the notes of each chord on the same four strings, and making each note move as little as possible when changing chords.

Before we begin, let's recap the interval formulas for the most common types of jazz guitar chords.

Major 7	1 3 5 7
Minor 7	1 b3 5 b7
7	1 3 5 b7
m7b5	1 b3 b5 b7

If you are not sure how to construct any of the following chords refer back to this table.

We will start the chord sequence with the following 'standard' Em7b5 shape although you could start with any comfortable voicing:

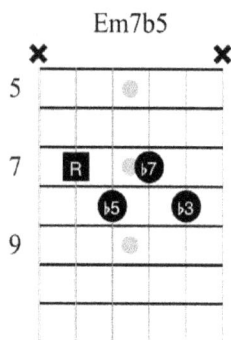

Take a moment to familiarise yourself with the location of each interval of the chord. Notice where the root (R), 3rd, 5th and 7th are located on the neck.

The goal is to move as few notes as possible between the Em7b5 and the following A7 chord while keeping to the same four strings.

If you have read Jazz Guitar Chord Mastery, you may already know the following chord shape for A7, but even so, try to form each chord interval by interval. This may be a little 'painful' at first, but the benefits will quickly become apparent.

The root of A7 is located on the 7th fret of the fourth string, but you may well see it more quickly on the 5th fret of the sixth string. (Try to learn the notes on the fourth string thoroughly as it will help greatly with your fluency).

Visualise the root note, A, and then add in the intervals that are required to form an A7 chord (a 3rd, 5th and b7). This is difficult, but be persistent and your skills will develop with time.

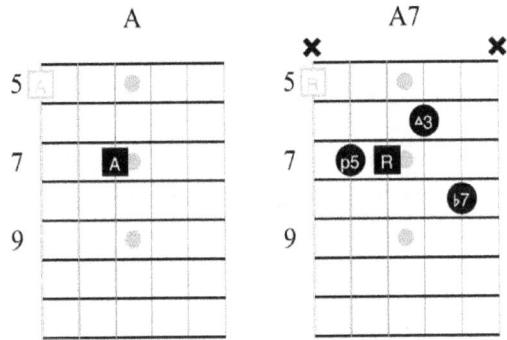

When we learn to see chord structures in terms of their intervals, certain things become very clear. For example, ask yourself, how would you change the previous A7 chord into an AMaj7 chord?

Study the table on the previous page and you will see that the only difference between A7 and AMaj7 is that A7 contains a *flattened* 7th (b7). If you raise the b7th of the A7 by a semitone, you create an AMaj7 chord voicing.

Compare the following:

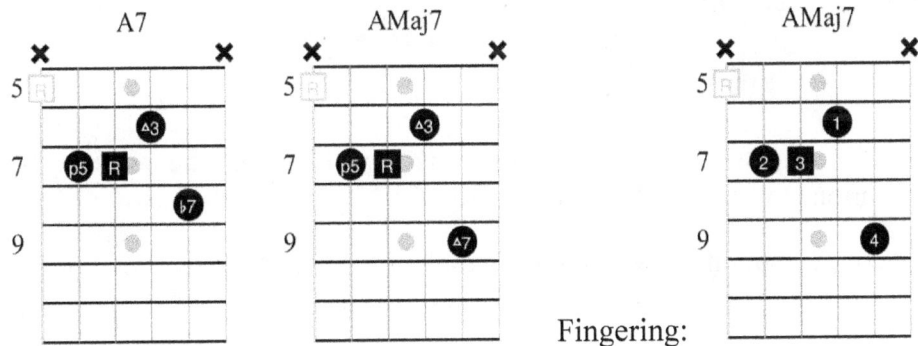

Fingering:

This is a bit of a stretch, but it's is a great Maj7 voicing.

Now, how would you turn the A7 voicing into an Am7 voicing? Study the table on the previous page again. All that changes is that the major 3rd (3) is flattened to become a minor 3rd (b3). This can be seen in the following diagrams:

A7   Am7

Em7b5   A7

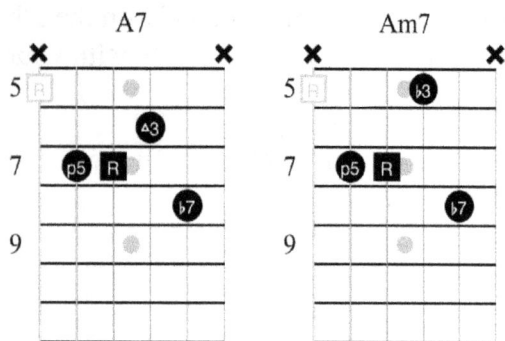

Again, this fingering is a little stretchy but it is another common m7 voicing. You can see that once you know a chord's formula and how to arrange these notes on the guitar, it is a very easy process to adjust shapes that you already know to produce many different chord types.

Let's get back to Bella!

Compare the chord voicings of Em7b5 and A7 and notice how similar they are.

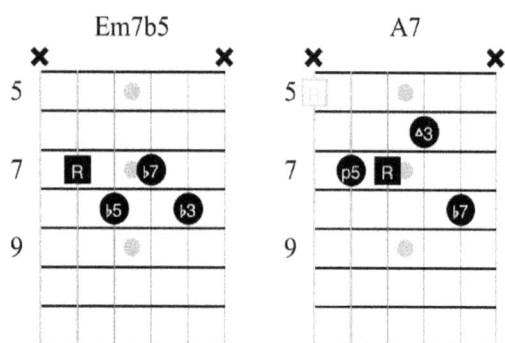

The only difference between these two chords is that is that the two *inside voices* of Em7b5 (the notes on the middle strings) have both fallen by a semitone to become the root and 3rd of A7.

The challenge for us it to learn to adjust our perception of the guitar neck each time a chord changes, presenting us with a new root note.

In other words, when the chord is Em7b5 we are viewing the fretboard in terms of its root note (E) and its relevant chord tones. As soon as the chord changes to A7, we must adjust our thinking so that we see the fretboard in terms of the new root note (A) and the intervals of A7. This process is quite mentally demanding, but it does get easier, and you will develop your skills in this book.

The chord after A7 is Cm7 (1 b3 5 b7).

Begin by finding the closest location of the root note (C) on the middle four strings:

```
          C
  ✗           ✗
  ┌─┬─┬─┬─┐
  ├─┼─┼─┼─┤
5 ├─┼C┼─┼─┤
  ├─┼─┼─┼─┤
7 ├─┼○┼─┼─┤
  ├─┼─┼─┼─┤
9 ├─┼○┼─┼─┤
  └─┴─┴─┴─┘
```

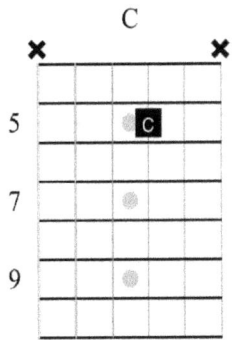

Next, we gradually build up the intervals of Cm7 around it.

Chords with a root note on the third string are often the hardest chords to visualise on the guitar. Most guitarists play chords with the roots on the sixth, fifth or fourth strings, so third-string roots can be a bit of a mystery to us.

It may help at first to think of the notes in the chord (C Eb G Bb) and place those on the neck first before thinking of intervals. Again, all I can say is that this does get easier, but it can be slow and frustrating at first. My advice is to try to enjoy the mental pain as this is your brain learning important and advanced information about the guitar.

We can build the intervals of Cm7 around the root in the following way:

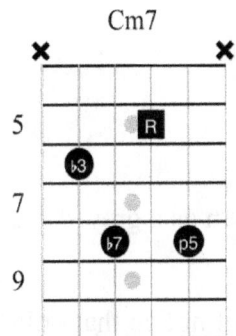

```
          Cm7
  ✗           ✗
  ┌─┬─┬─┬─┐
  ├─┼─┼─┼─┤
5 ├─┼R┼─┼─┤
  ├b3┼─┼─┼─┤
7 ├─┼○┼─┼─┤
  ├─┼b7┼p5┼─┤
9 ├─┼○┼─┼─┤
  └─┴─┴─┴─┘
```

Learn to recognise what a b3, 5, and b7 look like in relation to a third string root.

This chord may not be comfortable to play at first, but it is a fantastic sound once you get used to it.

Compare this Cm7 voicing to the previous A7 chord:

A7   Cm7

Cm7   F7

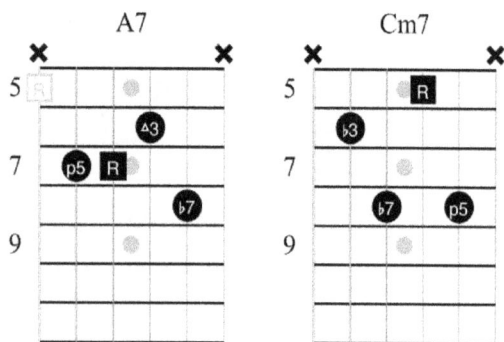

Here, only one note remains the same between the two chords, because there is a fairly pronounced key change at this point in the song. Even so, each note moves by only one semitone and even this small movement can be further reduced when we start to introduce substitutions and extensions later.

The final chord in the sequence is F7. The closest voicing of this chord is as follows:

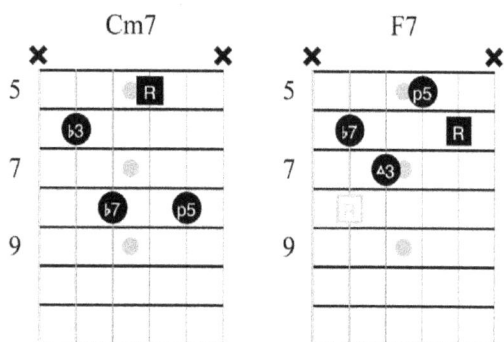

You may find it easier to view the root of this F7 chord as being on the fifth string. It is shown as a greyed out square for your reference.

Once again, compare the F7 to the previous Cm7 to see which voices have moved. You will notice that only two notes have changed. This change can be reduced to one note by playing an F9 chord instead of the F7, and we will look at this idea in the following chapter.

The past few pages have covered a huge amount of information and may seem quite daunting. The best way to internalise this approach is to get your hands dirty and actually practice it with a mindful approach.

How to Practice

This exercise is simple on paper, but it may take you a while to master.

Play the first chord of the sequence, Em7b5. Strum the chord and then pick each string individually. As you pick each string, say the name of each interval out loud. For example:

Example 1a:

The audio examples in this book are available for free download from www.fundamental-changes.com Simply click the 'Download Audio' link at the top of the page.

When you have played through the notes of Em7b5 and said their names out loud, pause and *visualise* the notes of the following chord (A7) on the fretboard. Before you move to A7, make sure you can *see* how the intervals of the Em7b5 chord you are holding change to become the intervals of A7. This may take time, but the idea is to see the new chord *before* you move from the one you're on. Notice which notes move and which notes stay the same.

Repeat this process for every chord in the sequence. Try not to see the sequence as chord 'shapes', like when you first learned to play, try to see it as intervals shifting and cascading down the fretboard. Of course, you may already know these chord shapes but focus on seeing the intervals in terms of each new root note.

Example 1b:

Let's move on to the next four bars of Bella.

Fm7		B♭7		E♭maj7		A♭7	
5		6		7		8	

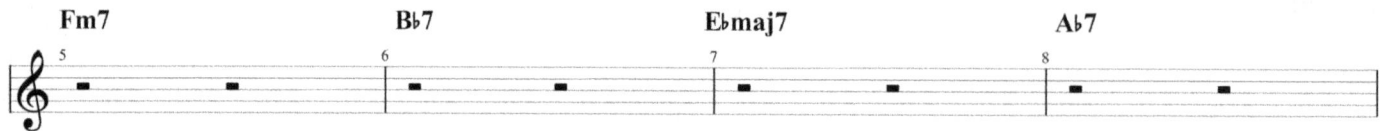

Each chord can be played in the following way:

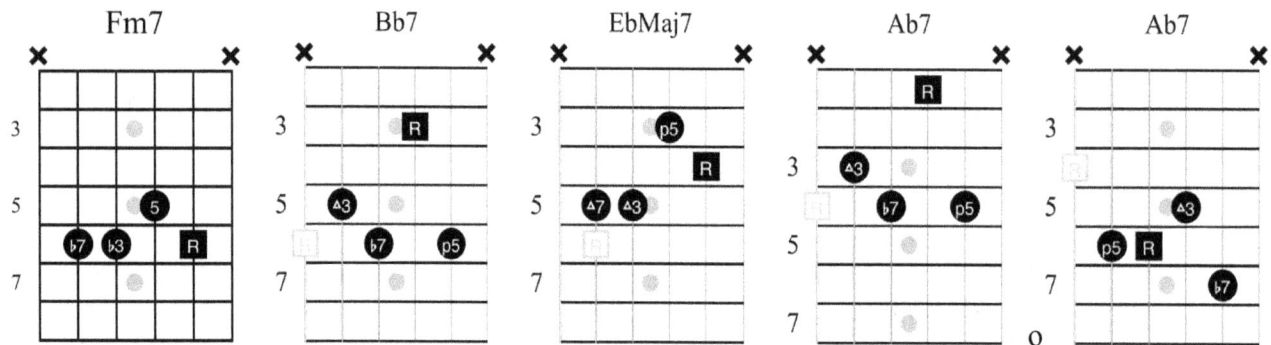

Approach these chord changes in the same way as before. Play the first chord and say the intervals out loud before visualising how each note changes to become an interval of the following chord. Only change chords when you are confident with what you are about to play.

Remember: try not to see chord shapes, try to view each chord as a set of changing intervals.

I have given two options for the final A7 chord. The first fits in more 'correctly' with the exercise because the voice leading is a bit closer, but it is a bit of a stretchy shape so you may wish to move back up the fretboard and use the second option. Developing a choice of voicings and learning to see the intervals in more than one place on the fretboard gives you a lot of freedom and allows you many creative options to use when you are comping jazz guitar.

By using a different voicing for A7 chord, the *next* chord will also be played with a different closest voicing, setting up a chain of events that will take you on a different pathway through the changes. Eventually, you will be able to play any voicing you choose and improvise freely with your choice of chord voicing.

When you are confident with closely voiced chords, you will start to experiment with voicings that 'jump' around the neck or across string groups, normally with the aim of keeping a particular melody note at the top of the chord.

The next four bars of Bella are written out here, one bar per chord. Be sure to practice this in the same way as example 1b.

Example 1c:

Play the through the complete first eight bars, and continue the process of strumming every chord once before picking each individual note and saying the interval names out loud. Visualise the next chord before moving your fingers.

Example 1d:

In the above example, it is easy to see how only one note moves between F7 and Fm7 in bars five and six.

Here are the next four bars of Bella arranged with tight voice leading on the middle four strings.

Example 1e:

Practice these four bars in the same way as before and put great emphasis on seeing how the intervals move between each chord.

Here is one route around the final four bars of the A section. As we start to run out of room at the bottom of the guitar notice how we start to ascend back up the neck

Example 1f:

Fmaj7 **Em7♭5** **A7** **Am7♭5** **D7**

```
Fmaj7      Em7b5    A7      Am7b5    D7
T  5        3        5       4        3
A  2        0        2       2        2
B  3        2        5       5        4
   3        1        4       3        3
```

There are a few challenging stretches here, but each shape will get easier over time. Some shapes will cause you to really adjust your wrist position or stick your elbow out. Experiment to find the most accessible position for you.

For now, don't worry too much about the awkward stretches, as we start to introduce substitutions, extensions and alterations we can avoid difficult fingerings (if we want to!) and increase the smoothness of the voice leading further.

To recap, here are the first sixteen bars of Bella by Barlight using voicings on the middle four strings. Notice that we play the minor ii V (Em7b5 – A7) a different way each time it occurs.

Example 1g:

```
Em7b5      A7       Cm7      F7
T  8        8        8        6
A  7        6        5        5
B  8        7        8        7
   7        7        6        6
```

```
Fm7        Bb7      Ebmaj7   Ab7
T  6        6        4        7
A  5        3        3        5
B  6        6        5        6
   6        5        5        6
```

Bbmaj7   Em7b5   A7   Dm7   Bbm7   Eb7

Fmaj7   Em7b5   A7   Am7b5   D7

In the next chapter, we look at how to use extensions, alterations and rootless voicings to smooth out the voice leading in each chord change.

Chapter Two: Extensions and Rootless Voicings

As I mentioned in the introduction, it is rarely necessary to play the root of the chord and often other intervals can be omitted too. The theory behind omitting notes is often taught academically and rigidly, with specific rules about which notes can be dropped in a chord and when it is acceptable to do so. The truth is that there are no hard and fast rules about which notes must be included. More often than not, the listener will subconsciously 'fill in the gaps' when strong voice leading is used, even when an important note such as the 3rd is omitted.

By omitting the root and occasionally other intervals too, we can access other notes that add richness and interest to our chordal textures. Usually, when a note such as the root is left out, it is replaced by another note, either a natural *extension* (9th, 11th or 13th) or by a chromatic *alteration* (b9, #9, b5 or #5).

These extensions and alterations are covered in great detail in my books Guitar Chords in Context and Jazz Guitar Chord Mastery, but the following table shows the most common choices for jazz chords. This list isn't exhaustive, extensions can be combined, and you should be aware of *enharmonic* notes such as a b5 being identical to the #11.

Chord Type	Formula	Common Extensions
Maj7	1 3 5 7	9 #11 13 (or 6)
m7	1 b3 5 b7	9 11
m7b5	1 b3 5 b7	b9 9 11
7 (unaltered)	1 3 5 b7	9 11 #11 13
7 (altered)	1 3 (5) b7	b9 #9 b5 (#11) #5 (b13)

There are no 'avoid' notes, but 13ths (or 6ths) need to be handled with care on minor chords. Chord ii will normally contain a natural 13 whereas chords iii and vi contain b13s. Consider these as special cases and something to study later.

One important substitution to know is that Maj7 chords are often played as 6 or 6/9 chords on the guitar. For example, instead of playing EbMaj7 in bar seven of Bella by Barlight, it is common to hear Eb6 (1 3 5 6) or Eb6/9 (1 3 6 9). Piano players may use different formulas to play 6, and 6/9 chords but these voicings work well on the guitar. Sometimes the 7th can be included in a 6/9 chord if the root is omitted although technically this would be a Maj13th chord.

A dominant 7 chord acting as a *functional* V7 chord (for example in a ii V I progression) can normally take any level of tension you care to add, although certain situations may heavily suggest a specific tension. One tension that it is normally okay to add to any functional dominant is the b9. The b9 is normally substituted for the root and is probably the most common tension used in jazz.

The best way to learn these sounds is to study how they are used in rhythm guitar parts. The 'rules' of harmony are subjective, so if someone tells you about a rule of music, don't discount it, but use it as a solid foundation from which to explore. Most things in music are about context; it is always possible to play something that would be considered a 'wrong' note by most theory experts if it is done at the right point in the song. This skill comes down to rhythm, phrasing and conviction.

The important thing to realise about any 'altered' note choices I use in this book is that they are not chosen at random. In other words, each note choice occurs because it provides good voice leading between chords.

Let's study some 'extension and alteration' possibilities on the first four bars of Bella by Barlight. We will begin with a common Em7b5 voicing.

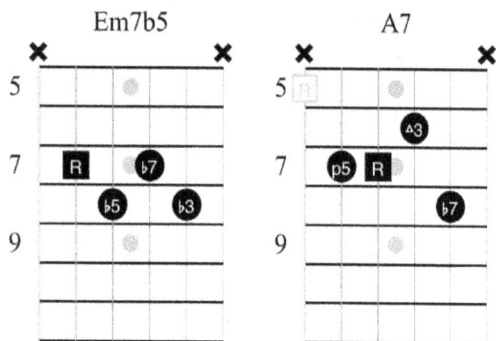

In the previous chapter, two notes changed between the chords of Em7b5 and A7. Let's look at how we can further reduce the amount of moving voices.

To refresh your memory, here are the first four bars of Bella by Barlight:

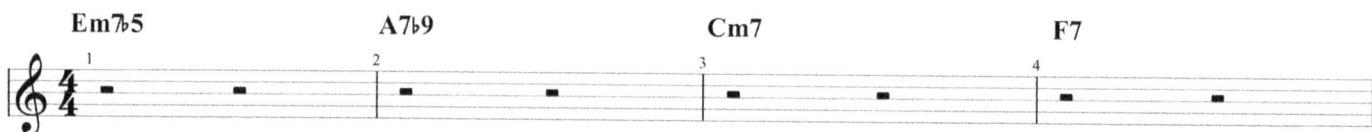

Despite the A7 not resolving to a D chord, it is still considered part of a ii V progression and will, therefore, accept some tension. Also, the *melody* of the original tune at this point contains a b9 note (Bb), so it can be appropriate to reflect that tension in the chord part.

The Em7b5 chord *already contains the Bb* note (on the fourth string), so instead of moving down to the root of the A7 chord (A) as before, we can leave it where it is and *only* move the b7 of Em7b5 down to become the 3rd of A7. This is easier to understand when seen it in the following diagram.

Example 2a:

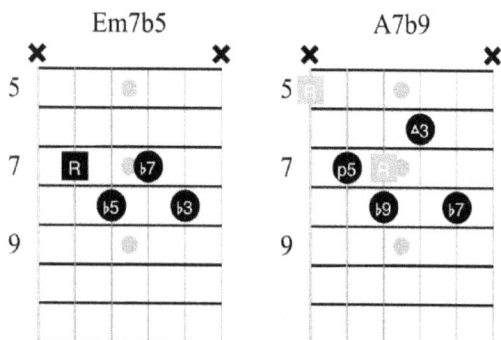

We have simultaneously introduced a rich, beautiful alteration to the A7 chord while also reducing the number of moving voices to create a tight, efficient musical harmony.

As with any chord, there are many extensions that can be added to the following Cm7 although in this case my first choice would be to stick with the unaltered voicing from Chapter One as it continues the stepwise voice leading:

Example 2b:

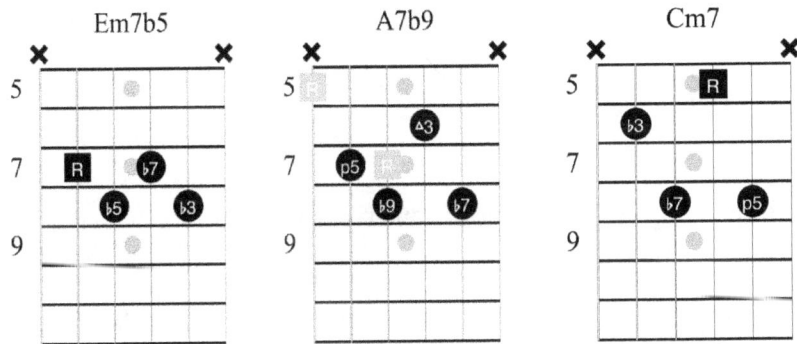

Notice how the note on the third string falls by a semitone on each chord.

9ths can be freely added to most dominant 7 chords, and by adding a 9th to the following F7, we can move from Cm7 to F9 by changing just one note. In the following diagram, you can see how we replace the root of the Fm7 chord (F) with the 9th (G):

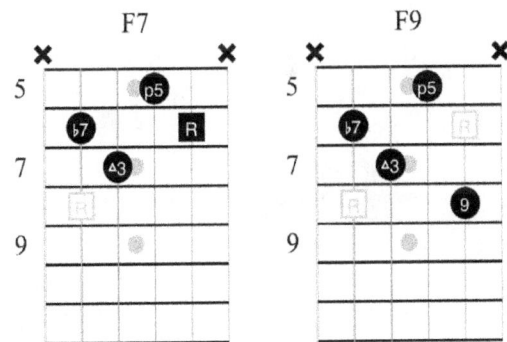

The 9th of F7 (G) is same note as the 5th of the previous Cm7 chord (G), allowing this note to remain unchanged over both chords. As you can see, only one note now changes between Cm7 and F9. The b7 of Cm7 (Bb) falls to the 3rd of F9 (A).

Example 2c:

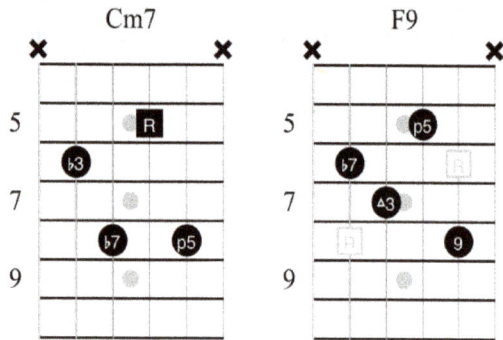

Of course, there are other extensions that could be used on the F7 chord, but right now we are focused on creating the smallest possible movements between chords.

Play through the first four bars of Bella, paying careful attention to the voice leading on each string. As before, try to visualise each interval and note change before you play it. Strum each chord before picking each note in turn and saying the intervals out loud.

It is very important to get into the habit of 'building' each chord from its constituent intervals whenever you change chord. Try not to memorise shapes; build every chord note by note by first placing the root, then other intervals.

Example 2d:

We can continue in a similar vein for the next four bars.

Fm7   Bb7   Ebmaj7   Ab7

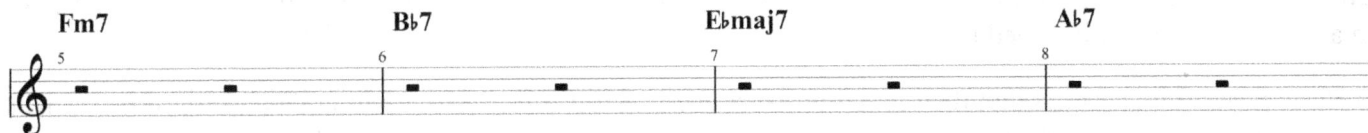

In the previous bar of F7, the root was replaced by the 9th. As seen in the table at the beginning of this chapter, the 9th is a great interval to play on both the F7 *and* the Fm7 chord, so let's leave it where it is for now.

Now the only note that changes between F9 and Fm9 is the 3rd (A). It must fall by a semitone to become the b3 of Fm9 (Ab).

Example 2e:

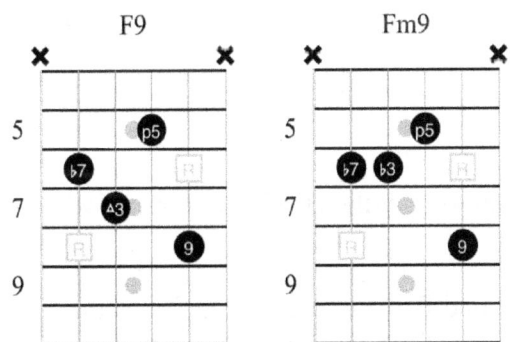

The next chord is a *functional* Bb7 that resolves in the following bar to the tonic EbMaj7. Once again, we can form a Bb7 voicing by changing just one note from the previous Fm9.

The question to always ask ourselves when finding routes through chord sequences is "what does each interval in this chord become when played over the root note of the next chord?"

The next diagram may look a little confusing at first, but it will help you to get 'inside the head' of a good jazz guitar player. The first diagram shows the intervals of Fm9 (the chord we are playing) over the root note of F. The second diagram shows the same notes, but this time they are viewed as intervals of Bb (the chord we are moving too).

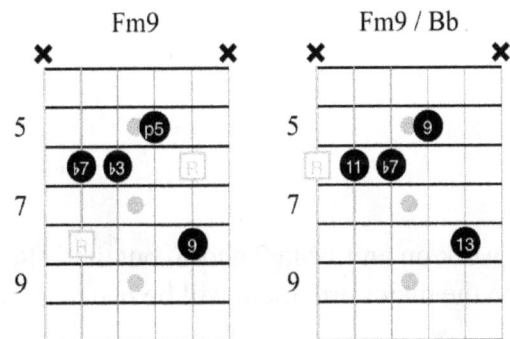

Look at the second diagram and compare it with the table at the start of the chapter. Which notes are 'acceptable' in a Bb7 chord and which need to change?

Well, the truthful answer is that they *all* could work well on the Bb7 chord. Playing this group of notes over a Bb bass note forms the chord Bb13sus4 (11 is the same as 4). We could continue playing this set of notes to create a tense harmony as the bass moves to Bb. However, at this point in the progression it is much stronger to hear the 3rd of the Bb7, so my suggestion is to drop the 11th to the 3rd in the following way:

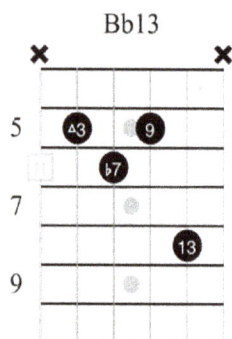

Bb13

It should be said that there are no 'rights or wrongs' here. You may wish to play the Bb13sus4 for a few beats before resolving to the Bb13.

As you can see, moving just one note of the Fm9 creates a rich, extended Bb13 chord that includes the 9th. Rootless voicings of chords are extremely useful on the guitar; by using just four notes we can create beautiful, advanced harmonies.

Remember: ask yourself on every chord change, 'Which notes can stay the same, which notes need to move?'

Let's move on to the EbMaj7 chord.

Look to see which intervals the notes of the current chord (Bb13) form against the Eb root note:

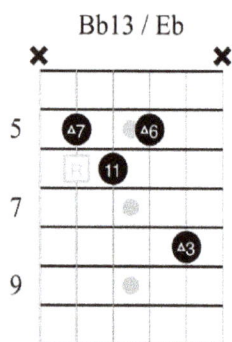

Bb13 / Eb

Refer back to the table. As you can see, the 7th, the 6th and the 3rd all work on an EbMaj7 chord, but the 11th will clash with the 3rd. The problem is that if we simply drop the 11th to the major 3rd, there will be *two* major 3rds in this voicing.

A good solution is to drop the 11th to the 3rd but *also* to drop the higher 3rd to the 9th creating a slightly unusual Maj13th chord (a Maj6 chord that includes the 7th):

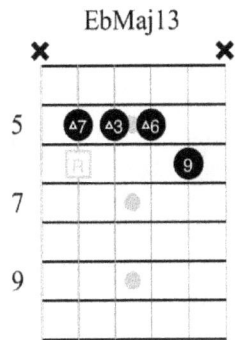

EbMaj13

(Guitar chord diagram: frets 5–9, notes Δ7, Δ3, Δ6 on 5th fret, R below, 9 on adjacent string)

Again, this is a rootless voicing that has slight tension due to the 7th in the bass. This is a great sound, but possibly a voicing to avoid if you're working in a duo with an inexperienced singer. If you need to play the root as the lowest note then you could opt for a more standard Eb6/9 chord:

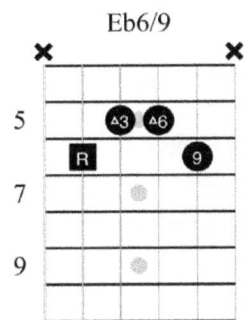

Eb6/9

(Guitar chord diagram: frets 5–9, notes Δ3, Δ6, R, 9)

The final chord of this section is Ab7. In *Bella by Barlight*, it is often played as an A7#11 (or 'Lydian Dominant') chord. Once again, see what intervals the current EbMaj13 chord tones form against the root of the next Ab7#11 chord:

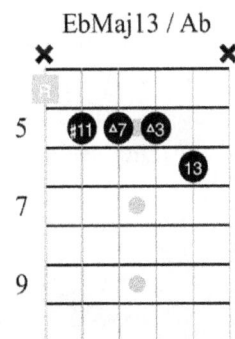

EbMaj13 / Ab

(Guitar chord diagram: frets 5–9, notes #11, Δ7, Δ3, 13)

This voicing already contains three intervals we can use for Ab7#11. The only note that needs to change is the 7th, which must fall by a semitone to the b7 (Gb):

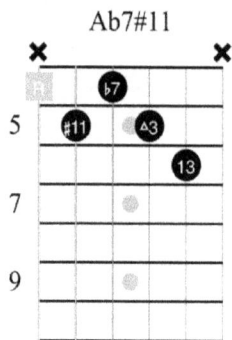

You may recognise this chord as a 'Hendrix' D7#9 shape, but over an Ab root it functions completely differently.

Recap the second four bars of Bella, playing each chord and then its intervals.

Example 2f:

Play smoothly through the first eight bars of the song and visualise the root notes of any rootless voicings. Notice how the top note of each chord remains unchanged for the first six bars. Compare this sequence to how you used to play these chords.

Example 2g:

Unfortunately, there isn't room in this book to analyse and discuss every chord change on Bella with diagrams and comparisons, so I have condensed following next eight bars into one line. Every chord has its intervals shown in the chord grids. It is your job to dissect and learn how every note functions in the sequence.

Pay attention to which extensions/alterations are used and why. If an extension is used, look to see which chord tone is being replaced.

Second Eight Bars of Bella by Barlight

Example 2h:

Eb7b9 FMaj9 Em7b5 A9 Am7b5b9

D7#5b9

Bbmaj6 Em7b5 A7b9 Dm11 Bbm9 Eb7b9 Fmaj9 Em7b5 A9 Am7b5b9 D7#5b9

The previous sequence shows just one route through the chord changes, in the next chapter we will discuss how to practice finding new pathways. For now, try to find new routes by adding different extensions on each dominant chord.

The chords to the B section of Bella by Barlight are as follows:

G7#5 Cm7

Ab7#11 Bbmaj7

Em7♭5   A7♭9   Dm7♭5   G7♭9

Cm7♭5   G7♭9   B♭mja7

Begin by finding the closest possible voicings for these chords while ignoring any chromatic alterations as we did in Chapter One. For example instead of G7b13, play a simple G7. One pathway could be played as follows:

Example 2i:

The first eight bars of this example contain just four chords, each one lasting two bars. Try to find a new voicing of the same chord in every second bar, and continue your voice leading from there. The following example should start you off on some new explorations.

Example 2j:

Incorporating this technique into your playing is explored in detail in Jazz Guitar Chord Mastery. As you can jump between any inversion of each chord, this concept requires very organised practice because each chord voicing directly affects the next.

The second line of example 2i contains three of the four common minor ii V movements on the middle four strings. Learn these thoroughly as they occur often.

As you begin to see how the R-7 chords function, begin to add extensions and alterations to the chords to form closer voice leading. The dominant 7 chords in the final eight bars are often played as 7b9 chords. Here's just one route through the changes.

Example 2k:

Work slowly through example 2k, mapping out the interval of each chord one by one. It may help to get a page of blank chord grids and write out each chord with the intervals marked on each note. Look carefully to see what voicing decisions I have made when moving from chord to chord.

You may once again wish to investigate the possibility of changing voicings in each bar. Changing voicing will take you to a new fretboard location and will directly affect the voicing of each chord that follows.

Remember! Avoid learning this progression as a series of chord shapes. Learn to see the intervals of one chord moving to new intervals in the subsequent chord. This is easier said than done, but it is possible to force yourself to see past the chord shape and focus only on the intervals. It takes a conscious effort to think like this, and you will find yourself getting mentally fatigued quite quickly. Your concentration and vision will improve with practice, so relax and enjoy the learning process. Take a lot of breaks.

Consciously build *every* chord from its component intervals *every* time. Don't think of chord shapes: build each chord, note by note by placing the root, then adding the rest of the intervals.

Chapter Three: Voicing Exercises and Practice Ideas

The previous chapters have helped you to build a solid pathway through the chord changes to Bella by Barlight using efficient voicing leading and by introducing alterations and extensions to help smooth the movement between each chord voice.

In this chapter, you will learn how to explore, expand and practice your own ideas for voice leading through chord changes. Throughout the following ideas, one concept should dominate your thinking: 'the closest note principle'. Always move between chords by changing the fewest number of notes.

The ideas in this chapter are once again taught in the context of Bella by Barlight, but they should be applied to every jazz tune you study.

The first idea to practice is simply to begin the chord progression with a different voicing. As each subsequent chord is formed by adjusting notes from the one previous, starting the progression in a different location will force you to take a different route through the changes. In turn, this dramatically improves your ability to quickly find chord intervals in different parts of the neck and drastically increases your vision and fluency on the guitar.

In the previous chapters we started the progression with this voicing of Em7b5:

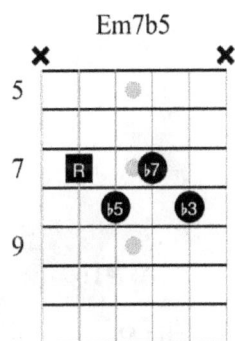

However, there is no reason that we have to use this voicing of Em7b5. Starting in a different location allows us to practice finding different routes through the changes. The following example shows a pathway through the first eight bars beginning with the following voicing of Em7b5.

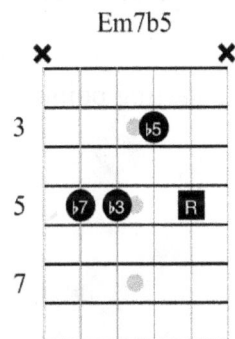

Example 3a:

Carefully analyse this chord sequence to make sure you understand every note choice before continuing through the rest of the chord progression.

There are four inversions of 'drop 2' Em7b5 chords that you should start from. Each one is a starting point to a different route through the chord sequence. These four voicings are as follows:

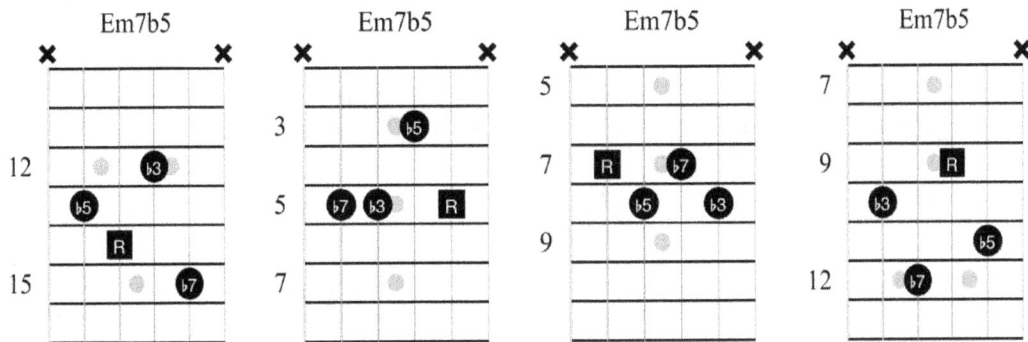

The first of the previous four voicings can be played an octave lower by using an open third string.

The next practice idea is to play through the sequence while the highest note in each chord either descends or remains at the same pitch. This approach has been part of all the exercises in this book so far because the harmony of Bella by Barlight tends to descend. However, being conscious of the melody (top) note of the chord will again allow you to open up the fretboard.

The following example starts with a high voicing of Em7b5 and descends melodically. As always, see each chord as a set of intervals and analyse each note choice. It's tricky to begin with, but it is the most beneficial way to practice.

Example 3b:

Continue this sequence throughout the whole chord progression. Work in short chunks of two to four bars at a time so that you don't burn out.

Next, try *only* allowing the top note to descend on each chord. It can be easy to run out of room on the fretboard so sometimes it is necessary to jump up an octave to the top of the guitar to continue.

Here are the first eight bars played with descending melody notes. Notice that the octave jump in bar five allows the melody note to fall in by step from D to C, albeit up an octave.

Example 3c:

Continue through the progression ensuring that the highest note of each chord descends with every change.

Jazz progressions often tend to descend harmonically as it is common for chords to move in intervals of 5ths and 4ths. A very useful approach to playing rhythm guitar is to force the voicings to *ascend* and move in the opposite direction to the harmony.

This ascending approach can be practiced in two ways. The first way is to ensure that the highest (melody) note of each chord ascends or remains constant on each chord change. The second way is to play *only* an ascending melody note on each chord.

The following example uses a combination of ascending and static melody notes. Work through this example before continuing the approach through the whole progression.

Example 3d:

Em7b5 | A7b5b9 | Cm7 | F7b9 | Fm9 | Bb7b9 | Ebmaj13 | Ab13#11

In the next example, the melody note ascends on each chord.

Example 3e:

Em7b5 | A7b9 | Cm13 | F9 | Fm7 | Bb7 | Ebmaj13 | Ab7

Continue this example through the whole progression. As you run out of frets, drop back down to the bottom of the guitar neck to continue the sequence. Work in small, two-bar phrases and take your time.

Another great way to practice chord and interval recognition is to limit your playing to small, five-fret areas of the guitar neck while keeping each voicing on the same four strings. This exercise is fairly demanding, so stick to simple '7th' voicings at first.

The first eight bars of Bella by Barlight can be played with R-7 voicings in the first to fifth frets as follows.

Example 3f:

Em7b5   A7   Cm7   F7

Fm7   Bb7   EbMaj7   Ab7

Em7b5   A7   Cm7   F7   Fm7   Bb7   Ebmaj7   Ab7

As your confidence builds, try to add simple extensions/alterations to the chords where you feel they are appropriate. One way to do this is shown below, but you should come up with as many approaches as you can.

Example 3g:

Em7b5   A7b9   Cm11   F7   Fm9   Bb7#5b9   Ebmaj9   Ab7#11

*OK, I cheated a little here and used an open string! However, making good music is always the priority, and I felt that this was the most appropriate voicing to use at this time.

To expand upon the previous exercise, divide the neck into different six-fret regions and play through the whole tune in a new region each week.

The following example shows one way to play the second eight bars of Bella between the sixth and tenth frets.

Example 3h:

Try to find as many closely voiced routes through the chords as you can in different positions. Begin by using simple R-7 voicings before introducing extensions and alterations.

* * *

There are many ways to voice chords on the guitar using different groups of strings and different structures. For example, we could use just the top four strings, the middle four strings, or indeed any other combination of strings we care to choose.

We will be looking in more detail at chord voicings on other string sets in later chapters, but bear in mind that each one of the previous voicing exercises could (and should) be applied to other types of voicing, the most common ones being 'drop 2' and 'drop 3' chords structures.

To get you started with other voicings, let's take a look at the first eight bars of Bella beginning with a *drop 3* voicing of the Em7b5 chord. Until now we have been mainly using *drop 2* voicings of each chord. For more explanation of this concept see my book Jazz Guitar Chord Mastery.

Em7b5 can be played as a drop 3 voicing in the following way:

Again, move through the chord sequence keeping each voice's movement as close as possible to the previous one while keeping the notes all on the same strings.

Example 3i:

Continue this approach throughout the whole song.

Using different voicings helps you see intervals on the neck instead of memorising individual chord shapes. Of course, if you already know these chord voicings you do need to make sure you see each chord in terms of its constituent intervals and not just as a pre-defined shape.

The goal of this book is to teach you to see inside each chord and learn to pick and choose which intervals you play. Memorising chord shapes is a good start, but if you don't see beyond shapes you are overlooking the more fundamental concepts of interval recognition, voice leading and spontaneous creativity. As your skills develop, you will begin to pick and choose which intervals you play when improvising rhythm guitar parts.

The following example begins with a drop 2 voicing on the top four strings and uses closely voiced chords to move through the 'C' section (bars 25-32) of Bella by Barlight with R-7 voicings. The following chord shapes are repeated in a descending sequence.

Example 3j:

Em7b5   A7b9

Em7b5   A7b9   Dm7b5   G7b9   Cm7b5   F7b9   Bbmaj7

The previous example is fairly predictable and follows the harmony down the neck. Try playing the same sequence but this time ascend the neck as shown.

Example 3k:

Em7b5   A7b9   Dm7b5   G7b9   Cm7b5

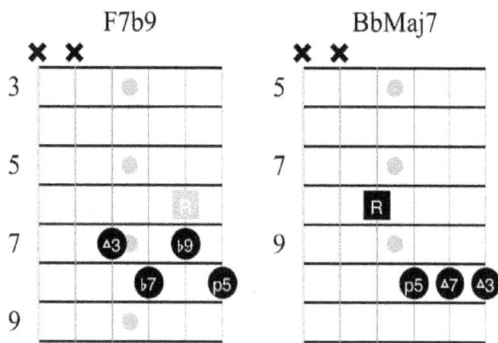

F7b9   BbMaj7

Em7b5   A7b9   Dm7b5   G7b9   Cm7b5   F7b9   Bbmaj7

Even with fairly simple chords, arranging the voicings so that they ascend the neck against a descending harmony is a beautiful, musical technique.

Finally for this section, here is a practice technique that is completely opposite to everything we have studied so far, but is a fantastic way to speed up your thinking and enhance your creativity.

The concept behind this practice technique is simply to keep the root of each chord on the same string while playing the same chord structures (drop 2, drop 3, etc.). This is fairly straightforward when the root of the chord is on the sixth, fifth or fourth string, but more challenging when the root is on the second or the third string.

To demonstrate, let's begin with the root of Em7b5 on the fifth string. We will then play through the first four bars of Bella by Barlight keeping the root of each chord on the same string. This means that we will be moving large distances and constantly reorganising our thinking.

This is should be quite an easy exercise, as you probably already know these voicings and the roots are all located on a familiar string.

Example 3l:

Em7b5   A7   Cm7   F7

etc…

When you practice, consciously build *every* chord you play from its component intervals *every* time you change chord. Don't think of chord shapes; build the chord note by note by first placing the root then the 3rd, the 5th and finally the 7th. Later, when you are adding/substituting extensions or alterations you should be able to immediately see which intervals you wish to replace.

Try the exercise again, but this time keep the root of each chord on the *second* string. Remember, don't memorise chord shapes! Find the root on the second string each time and build the chord up from the root.

Example 3m:

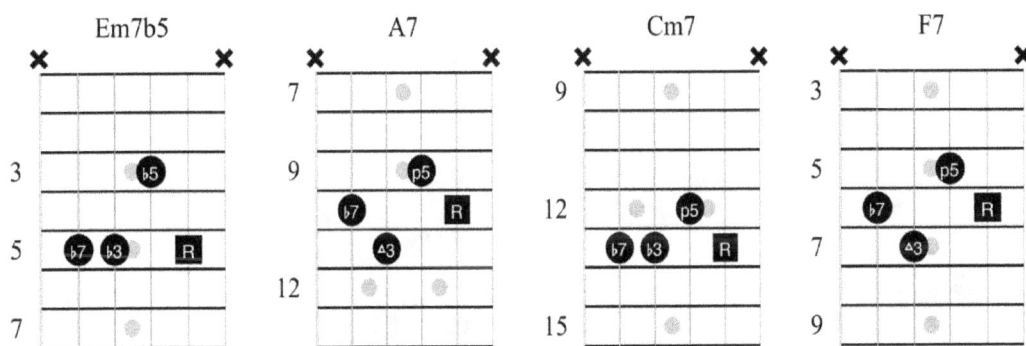

Em7b5   A7   Cm7   F7

Most people find the previous voicings much harder to visualise as they are not as familiar with the intervals on the guitar when viewed from a second-string root. Continue through the whole progression using simple R-7 chords ensuring that you keep the root of each chord on the second string. You will quickly master the four main types of jazz chord (Maj7, m7, 7, and m7b5) played as drop 2 voicings with second-string roots.

As your confidence develops, you may start to find yourself seeing chord shapes, not individual intervals. If this happens, try to build the chords in a different order. For example, place the 3rd of the chord first, then the 7th, then the 5th and then finally the root. Keep these exercises fresh and challenging in order to develop choice and freedom in your playing.

The next stage is to use *rootless* voicings while still visualising the root of each chord on the second string. This is a very challenging exercise.

To begin, play *every chord* with a 9th replacing the root. Each chord could, in theory, be played with a natural or b9 depending on its context. Use your ears to help you decide which to use.

Here are the first eight chords of Bella played with 9th voicings that omit the root. Each string's root is visualised on the second (B) string.

Example 3n:

Continue this idea through the full Bella by Barlight chord progression.

Exercises like this really help us to isolate specific intervals and to vastly improve our fretboard knowledge as we must visualise both the root note *and* its replacement. We can extend this exercise further to target 11ths and 13ths too.

You will have noticed by now that placing the root on the second string means that all the other chord tones also remain on the same strings, i.e., the 3rd is always on the fourth string and the 5th is always on the third string when we use drop 2 chord voicings.

Play through chord sequence again, but this time replace the 3rd of each chord with a natural 11th. The chords sound unusual and there are some awkward fingerings, but it's a great exercise to help us see the fretboard. Take your time over these tasks and work in small, one- or two-bar chunks.

Example 3o:

EMaj7(sus4)   A7sus4   Cm7(sus4)   F7sus4

etc.

Finally, replace every 5th with a 13th.

Example 3p:

Em7b5b13   A13   Cm13   F13

etc.

Altering chords in this way works well with drop 2 chords with their roots on the second string although some shapes may be impossible to play when the root is placed on the third or fourth string, so just do what you can. If a voicing is unplayable, simply play the R-7 chord or adjust a different note.

It will take time to develop confidence and vision with these exercises, but when you begin to improve, try to do the same set of exercises using drop 2 chords with the root on the *third* string.

Your starting point for these exercises could be the following voicing of Em7b5:

Em7b5

If you think you have run out of starting points, you may want to refresh your memory with the essential chord voicings in Jazz Guitar Chord Mastery.

As an extension to these exercises, try repeating the substitution ideas above, but return to limiting your fret range. For example, play each chord as a 9th (replacing the root) but keep your playing within a pre-defined six-fret span on the neck.

The following example shows how to play the first eight chords of Bella by Barlight as 9ths within the range of first five frets.

Example 3q:

Repeat this exercise in other limited ranges on the guitar.

The exercises shown in this chapter can and should be repeated with any other chord structures you know and can be applied to any jazz progression. They provide a solid grounding voice leading jazz guitar.

Chapter Four: Secondary Dominants

"Any chord can be preceded by a dominant chord played a 5th above".

Secondary dominant chords are often used in jazz harmony, and they give us many opportunities to create interesting and complex chord progressions. Let's begin by exploring how to form secondary dominants in detail with some simple chord voicings.

The first exercise teaches us how to play a dominant chord on the 5th of every chord in a harmonised C Major scale. A dominant chord on the 5th of a chord is called a *secondary dominant* as it is secondary to the original dominant chord of the key.

The harmonised scale of C Major can be played with drop 2 voicings in the following way:

Example 4a:

Next, we need to learn what the secondary dominant of each of these chords is. They are shown in the following table:

Chord	Secondary Dominant
CMaj7	G7
Dm7	A7
Em7	B7
FMaj7	C7
GMaj7	D7
Am7	E7
Bm7b5	F#7 *

* You may be expecting the secondary dominant for Bm7b5 to be F7, but it is not. Secondary dominants are always formed on the *perfect* 5th of the root note, so we ignore the fact that m7b5 chords contain a b5 (in the case of Bm7b5 the b5 is is F, a diatonic note in the scale of C), and we use the *perfect 5th* (F#) even though this is not diatonic to the key of C.

We can now place a secondary dominant chord before each chord in the key of C Major.

Example 4b:

*Warning! Once again, the visual nature of the guitar neck is our enemy here. It is easy to get caught up playing patterns of shapes as you can see above. Instead of thinking 'all I have to do is move a dominant chord across a string' make sure you go through the mental process of finding the dominant note of each chord. Say each one out loud without looking at your guitar to make sure you are not relying on visual patterns of root movements.

At this stage, the overall effect is to create a kind of 'classical' feel. Essentially (with the exception of the diatonic G7), each secondary dominant introduces notes into the progression that are not in the original key, and classical musicians would treat this sequence as eight mini-modulations or key changes.

Now that you understand how a secondary dominant chord functions, we can repeat the previous sequence with better voice leading by using four-note voicings on a specific string group.

Let's begin with drop 2 voicings on the top four strings. It is important that you know these voicings. If you are in any doubt refer to *Jazz Guitar Chord Mastery.*

Example 4c:

By using secondary dominants and good voice leading, even a diatonic scale starts to sound musical and interesting although this is still just the tip of the iceberg.

If you are confident with drop 2 chord shapes and are adept at 'thinking' through this dominant cycle, try to see beyond the chord shapes to the individual intervals in each chord. However, this exercise is quite mentally demanding so your first priority should be to develop instant mental recall of each dominant chord.

Test yourself:

What is the secondary dominant of Am7?

What is the secondary dominant of Em7?

What is the secondary dominant of Bb7?

If your answers are not instant, keep practicing until you can answer immediately. It can be useful to make flash cards to randomly test yourself.

The previous example used tight voicing leading, but, in general, the voicings tended to descend. In Chapter Three we discussed different ways to explore chord sequences, so let's briefly apply some of those techniques before moving on.

As the voicings in the previous example descended, let's make the top note either stay the same or ascend the neck. The first two bars are done for you, but you should continue through the sequence yourself. It's essential practice.

Next, stay within a five- or six-fret range.

Work through the practice ideas in Chapter Three using this sequence of chords. Try them with different voicings and on different string sets. Remember, the main options are:

1) The top note remains the same or ascends on each chord

2) The top note ascends on each chord

3) The top note stays the same or descends on each chord

4) The top note descends on each chord

5) Play within a pre-defined fret range

6) Keep the root of each voicing on the same string

Focus on using just the top four strings for now, but you may want to return here later to apply these practice ideas to secondary dominant chords that use different voicings on different string sets.

Next, let's begin to add some altered tensions to each dominant chord. As each secondary dominant chord acts as a functional (resolving) dominant we can add as much tension as we like to each one.

We will start by replacing the root of each dominant chord with a b9 interval while using drop 2 voicings on the top four strings.

Example 4d:

This example beautifully illustrates a concept called the *diminished substitution*. Playing a diminished 7 chord on the 3rd of a dominant chord will always form a rootless 7b9 chord. For example,

C#Dim7 over A7 = A7b9.

D#Dim7 over B7 = B7b9.

Work through the previous example again and make sure you can see that when you raise the root of any '7' chord by a semitone, you form a 7b9 chord. This can also be seen as playing a diminished 7 chord (1 b3 b5 bb7) on the 3rd of the original dominant 7 chord.

Let's repeat the exercise but this time we will also add a 9th to each of the chords from the original diatonic scale. Bear in mind that chord iii (Em7) and chord vii (Bm7b5) both harmonise to have b9s, not natural 9ths.

Example 4e:

Finally, let's alter each dominant chord in a different way and play each one with a #5 (b13) by raising the 5th by a semitone. Isolating chromatic alterations in this way is a great way to learn to see intervals and hear their effect. To keep things simple, I will revert back to playing R-7 voicings on each diatonic chord.

Adjusting the 5th of each dominant chord is a little trickier, so to help you, here are the four dominant 7 chord shapes that we will be using. Find the 5th in each one and simply raise it by a semitone to access the #5 (b13).

When you're confident with the location of each 5th, go through the same diatonic chord progression and play each secondary dominant chord with a #5(b13).

Example 4f:

Repeat the exercise and play each secondary dominant chord with a #5 *and* a b9.

Try starting the previous exercises from each of the four different voicings of the CMaj7 chord:

Each time you should be able to find a new way around the changes.

Apply the exercises in this chapter to different chord voicings such as drop 2 and drop 3 chords with roots on the fifth and sixth string. For more voicing ideas check out my book Jazz Guitar Chord Mastery.

It is very important that you do the previous exercises in different keys. Begin your studies by working with the harmonised scale of Bb Major:

I	ii	iii	IV	V	vi	vii
BbMaj7	Cm7	Dm7	EbMaj7	F7	Gm7	Am7b5

Play the exercises in the keys of Eb, F and G Major before exploring minor keys.

Soon we will start to apply secondary dominant chords to real life jazz chord progressions, but first there are a few more important concepts that are important to understand.

The first concept is that you can add a ii chord to any secondary dominant. For example, take the following progression:

Fmaj7   Gmaj7   Am7

We have seen how to add a secondary dominant to each chord to create the following progression:

Fmaj7   D7   Gmaj7   E7   Am7

We can precede each of the secondary dominant chords with a ii chord to form a ii V I progression into the following diatonic chord.

The ii chord of a dominant 7 chord is built on the 5th, so the ii chord that precedes D7 is Am7.

One important thing to keep in mind is the chord *quality* that the secondary dominant chord is *resolving* to. If the secondary dominant chord resolves to a *major* chord we normally use a *m7* ii chord. If the secondary dominant resolves to a *minor* chord, we normally use a *m7b5* chord.

This ii V I movement is illustrated in the following diagram:

	Major ii V I			*Minor ii V I*		
FMaj7	Am7	D7	GMaj7	Bm7b5	E7	Am7
Diatonic Major	iim7	S.D.	Diatonic Major	iim7b5	S.D.	Diatonic Minor

S.D. = Secondary Dominant.

The ii chord built on the 5th of D7 is Am7. It is a m7 chord because it is resolving to a *Maj7* chord in bar three.

The ii chord built on the 5th of E7 is a m7b5 chord because it is resolving to a *m7* chord in bar five.

When resolving to the diatonic vii m7b5 chord (Bm7b5 in the Key of C) the ii chord can sound a bit funny. Don't worry about this for now and work through the following exercise using barre chords with roots on the fifth and sixth strings as you did in example 4b.

Example 4g:

Every other bar now forms a ii V progression resolving into the following diatonic chord.

Looking at the previous example, it is easy to see how far we have come from the simple diatonic chord progression at the beginning of this chapter, but once again this is just a starting point for your own in-depth studies. Begin by playing the previous progression with tight voice leading on the top four strings of the guitar as you did earlier.

Example 4h:

The example above compresses the chords into eight bars, but don't worry about the timing for now. Take as long as you need to understand and internalise the concept of adding a 'ii V' before each diatonic chord.

There is not enough room in this book to take you through all the permutations of alterations and extensions that can be added to each chord, not to mention voicing these chords in different inversions and locations on the guitar.

Don't rush and always try to look beyond the chord shapes to see the intervals in each chord – don't just memorise each shape. The following is a long list of options, so be prepared to work these ideas into your practice over a period of months and years, not just hours and days. Before you approach the following list, keep reading through this chapter to see how secondary dominants can be used in a musical context.

- Play each secondary dominant chord with a b9 replacing the root.

- Play each secondary dominant chord with a #5 replacing the fifth.

- Play each secondary dominant chord with both the b9 and the #5.

- Play each secondary dominant chord with a b5 replacing the fifth.

- Play each secondary dominant's ii chord with a 9th (or b9 depending on its function) replacing the root.

- Play each chord from the original diatonic progression with a 9th (or b9) replacing the root.

- Logically work through a process of combining the previous ideas.

- Begin from each of the four different inversions of the CMaj7 chord and ascend/descend for each change.

- Begin from each of the four inversions of other types of voicing, for example, drop 3 voicings.

- Work on different string groups beginning from each of the four voicings of CMaj7.

- Practice these ideas in different keys.

Musical Application

Secondary dominants and their associated ii chords can be used almost any time you change chords. For example, take the first four bars of Bella by Barlight.

The first two bars of Bella already form a ii V that looks like it should resolve to Dm7 although there is actually a key change and we move to Cm7. It is possible to use secondary dominant techniques on an existing ii V chord progression, but it is easier to learn by applying to chords that aren't already a 5th apart. In the above progression, the A7 to Cm7 is a prime candidate.

The following chart shows how to work *backwards* from the Cm7 to add the secondary dominant and then its ii chord.

The secondary dominant of C is G7, and the ii would *normally* be Dm7b5 because we are resolving to a C *minor 7* chord. However, there is a little anomaly here that you should be aware of. I would advise that you use a Dm7 chord as the ii, not a Dm7b5.

The reason for this is that the A7 chord before Cm7 contains the note A, but the Dm7b5 contains the note Ab (Ab is the b5 of D). The Ab sounds a bit awkward after the A7 in the previous bar. By playing the ii chord as Dm7 we avoid this issue entirely as Dm7 contains the note A as a natural 5th. This isn't to say you *can't* play Dm7b5, it just needs a bit of care.

Example 4i:

Play through this sequence with simple root position chords in the following way. Pay careful attention to the rhythm of bar two, as the rhythmic phrasing of the newly introduced chords is important. For added 'smoothness' try playing each dominant chord with a 7#5 tension.

We can add a secondary dominant before the Fm7 in bar five. I have used a dominant 13 chord here as the 13th of C (A) is the same note as the major 3rd of F7 and I didn't want to highlight the important change from F7 to Fm7 too early in the tune.

Example 4j:

Now we have seen how these secondary dominants work in context we can use some tight voice leading to make them flow more musically.

The following voicings are played on the middle four strings of the guitar, but you should explore other regions and permutations too. As the harmony now starts to become quite dense, you may at first wish to omit the ii chord of each secondary dominant and begin by playing the secondary dominant on beat three of bars two and four.

Example 4k:

The middle eight bars of Bella are also prime candidates for the secondary dominant treatment, as each chord is held for two bars.

The chord sequence is as follows:

Even though the movement from G7#5 to Cm7 is already a V – I progression, we can add a ii V secondary dominant sequence in bar two. We will also add secondary dominants to the Ab7 and the BbMaj7 and play a secondary dominant in bar eight as if we were going to continue to the Em7b5 chord in the following bar.

The resulting progression is:

Play through with simple root position chords before arranging the chords with good voice leading.

Example 4l:

Example 4m:

Example 4n:

Work very slowly through the above progression to make sure you understand how every extension and alteration is played on each chord.

You might not have been expecting to see the G7#5b9 chord at the beginning of example 4m, but it is a perfectly acceptable (and musical) choice because the G7 to Cm7 movement in the progression is a functional resolution. The b9 note (Ab) becomes the b5 of the following Dm7b5 ii chord.

An important thing to notice is that this G7#5b9 tension is created using a simple chord substitution. The first voicing in example 4m is clearly an Fm7b5 chord so remember that playing a m7b5 chord on the b7 of a dominant chord gives you the intervals b7, 3, #5, and b9.

This idea is summarised in the following table:

Notes of Fm7b5	F	Ab	Cb (B)	Eb (D#)
Interval formed against a G root note	b7	b9	3	#5

This is a very handy substitution to use as both a chordal and melodic idea; try playing an Fm7b5 arpeggio over a functional (resolving) G7 chord when you solo.

Find as many ways as you can to play the middle eight bars of Bella by Barlight on the guitar. Experiment by adding your own extensions and tensions, especially on the dominant chords. Play the changes in as many different places as you can while focusing on good voice leading between each chord. The four drop 2 voicings of G7 on both the four middle strings and the four top strings are a great place to start before moving on to drop 3 chords with roots on the fifth or sixth strings.

Remember that you don't *have* to play the written tensions and it can be a good idea to begin by ignoring them entirely. Play the first chord as a G7 and ignore the #11 on the Ab7 chord. The #11 is often played as it reflects the melody note of the tune at that point, but you don't have to play it if you don't want to.

For practice ideas, flick back to Chapter Three and work through a few of the suggestions there.

Above all, don't worry about getting everything perfectly correct at this stage. The thing to take from this chapter is the *concept* of secondary dominant chords and their associated ii chords.

It is great to test yourself away from your guitar. Give yourself a root note and see how quickly you can find its secondary dominant chord and it's ii chord. Again, flash cards can help here. For example:

Find the secondary dominant ii V progression for the chord Bm7.

The V of Bm7 is F#7.

The ii of F#7 is Cm7b5.

What are the secondary dominant ii V sequences for the following chords:

EMaj7, D7, Gm7, Fm7b5, C#m7?

Do you prefer the sound of a iim7b5 – V7 or a iim7 – V7 when resolving to a dominant 7 chord?

If the resolution chord is G7, do you prefer Am7b5 – D7 – G7, *or* Am7 – D7 – G7? How about A7#11 – D7 – G7?

There are no right or wrong answers. I'm just trying to encourage you to find your own voice. Experiment with these ideas and the answers will come to you.

Look for other points in Bella by Barlight where you can use secondary dominants, and try the ideas in this chapter out in different keys and with different tunes. There's a lifetime of exciting study to be had, and no single book can give you all the answers.

Chapter Five: The Tritone Substitution

The tritone (or 'b5') substitution is a fairly simple, yet essential musical concept frequently used by jazz musicians.

A tritone is the name given to the distance of three tones. Three tones above any note forms a b5 interval.

The concept is as follows:

Any functional dominant 7 chord can be substituted for another dominant 7 chord built on the b5 of the original chord.

Let's take a look at this idea in action.

Consider the following sequence that occurs in the final section of Bella:

The A7(b9) is a functional dominant chord that resolves to Dm7b5.

The tritone substitution rule says that we can play a dominant chord on the b5 of A7.

The b5 of A7 (three tones above) is the note Eb.

So we can play the chord Eb7 in place of the A7b9 chord to create the following chord sequence:

Notice how the root movement between each chord now falls in semitones. E – Eb – D.

This idea works even if the bass player plays the original root note (A) while we play the tritone substitution on the guitar. All that happens is we introduce some interesting altered tensions to the original A7 chord.

The following table shows you which alterations are created when playing an Eb7 over an A root note.

Notes of Eb7	Eb	G	Bb	Db/C#
Interval formed against an A root note	b5	b7	b9	3

As you can see, we retain the essential and character-defining 3rd and b7 of the A7 chord but we introduce the chromatic tensions b5 (#11) and b9. Quick calculation of the tritone substitution is essential when improvising with chords.

What are the tritone substitutions of the following chords?

G7, F7, Bb7, E7, and D7.

The way I calculated these substitutions when I didn't immediately know the answer was to first find the *perfect* fifth and then lower it by a semitone. For example, my mental process went something like this:

What it the tritone substitution of G7?

The fifth of G7 is D and a semitone below D is Db, so the tritone substitution for G7 is Db7.

Eventually this process will become as quick and unconscious as knowing that $2 + 2 = 4$.

The final eight bars of Bella by Barlight form a descending sequence of ii V I progressions in three different keys, eventually resolving to the tonic chord of BbMaj7. They can be seen in the following diagram:

The Dm7b5 functions as both the I chord for the Em7b5 – A7b9 sequence and as the ii chord in the following ii V I progression. The same is true for the Cm7b5 chord.

We can play a tritone substitution on every single dominant chord in the above progression to form the following sequence. Use simple root position chords on the fifth string to play through the following progression.

Example 5a:

As with secondary dominants, we can place ii chords before each new b5 (tritone) substitution. The ii chord is a fifth above the root of the new V7 chord. For example, the ii chord of Eb7 is Bbm7.

These substitutions are shown below.

This sequence can be played with 'basic' chord voicings on the guitar in the following way. Notice that I am using '9' chords instead of '7' chords to provide smoother voice leading on each tritone substitutions.

Example 5b:

At this point, we need to mention a very important consideration regarding the piece of music we are playing. While the above set of substitutions are 'theoretically' correct, they will not always work perfectly with the melody of the tune. Get yourself a Real Book chart of Stella by Starlight, and examine the melody of this section. In the first two bars of the above extract, the melody is as follows:

In the A7b9 bar, the melody contains the b7, R and b9 of A7b9. With the substituted tritone ii V chords above, the new harmony is:

It now becomes clear that there are a couple of problems with this reharmonisation of A7b9. The note A on beat one forms a major 7th against the Bbm7 chord, and the note G now forms a natural 6th. Record yourself playing the melody and then play the substituted chords to hear this clash.

While this b5 substitution is not 'technically' wrong, this example teaches us a very important and valuable lesson. The melody of the tune will always dictate what substitutions you can use.

While the above substitutions may not compliment the melody, they may be good choices to play under the soloist, or if the melody happened to be different.

So if the secondary dominant chord and its ii chord don't work in this specific example, how can we alter the substitution to take account of the melody?

One possibility is to simply omit the Bbm7 chord. It is possible to see the melody notes (A and G) as belonging to the Em7b5 in the previous bar. You could play these two bars as follows:

Example 5c:

If we were desperate to harmonise the note G in bar two, we could apply a technique commonly used in jazz and substitute the Bbm7 for a Bb7(#9). By swapping the minor chord for a dominant chord it allows us to use the tritone substitution of E. This means that we could use an E7#9 chord to harmonise the G on beat two:

Example 5d:

How to arrive at using an E7#9 will be explained later so don't worry about it for now.

A similar issue occurs in the following two bars where Abm7 and Db9 are substituted for the G7b9. See if you can spot the clashes in the following:

The note F forms a 13th against the m7 chord and in this context it is dissonant. A simple fix is to play the Abm7 chord as an Ab13 chord. In jazz, m7 chords are often substituted by dominant 7 chords (and in particular, 7#9 chords). This is explained in Chapter Six.

For now, a solution to the above clash could be played as follows:

Example 5e:

The previous three examples are included to show that the most important consideration when using chord substitutions is always the melody of the tune.

If we play chords under the melody, we need to be very careful that a 'theoretically correct' substitution is not going to clash with the melody note at that time. Even if a substitution is theoretically correct, if it clashes undesirably with the melody *it is wrong*.

We have more freedom when playing chords under a solo, as momentary clashes are much less important. However, before you go adding complex and distant substitutions to your rhythm guitar parts, please consider the experience and ability of your band mates, and the genre of music you are playing. What is appropriate for modern jazz may not be appropriate in a swing tune.

As mentioned earlier, the theory behind the substitutions above is explained in the following chapters, so don't panic if you haven't managed to follow every step.

The examples that follow in this book teach you substitution possibilities in an organised way, but please note that they disregard any melodic considerations. The examples are based on the changes to Bella by Barlight, but they may not all be appropriate when played with the tune's melody.

Let's now return to the earlier progression of secondary dominants and see how it could be played using close voice leading on different strings. Here is that progression once again to refresh your memory.

Example 5f:

Example 5g:

Tritone Substitutions on Secondary Dominants

Tritone substitutions can also be used with secondary dominant chords that have been added to the original chord progression. Refresh your memory of the first four bars of Bella by Barlight:

Let's begin by adding a secondary dominant chord and its ii chord to the Cm7 in bar three, just as we did in example 4i:

Next, let's replace the secondary dominant chord (G7) for *its* tritone substitution, Db7.

As you can see, we have now created the characteristic descending semitone movement from Dm7 down to Cm7 (D, Db, C).

Example 5h:

Next, instead of playing Dm7, *we can replace it with the ii chord of the b5 substitution (Abm7). *This will not work well when played with the original melody to the tune.*

Our progression becomes:

This can be played in the following way.

Example 5i:

Notice how I have used a D9 and a Cm11 to smooth the voice leading.

If you want to get really adventurous there's nothing stopping you from reintroducing the Dm7 chord before the Abm7:

Example 5j:

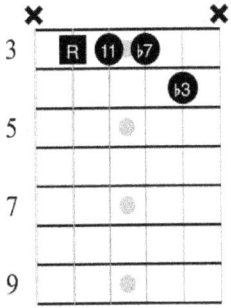

Cm11

The A7#5 is suggested because the #5 of A7 (E# / F) chord becomes the b3 (F) of the following Dm7 chord. You can also play the A7 chord with no alterations or with the b9 as written in the original song.

This is a lot of chords in a short space of time, but it does show what becomes possible with substitutions. Always keep in mind the tune's melody notes when you are exploring these ideas, although if you are playing this many chords so quickly, clashes are often fleeting and fairly insignificant.

Let's base our voice leading examples on the chord sequence from example 5i as the tritone substitution of the secondary dominant chord and its preceding iim7 chord are enough to be working with for now.

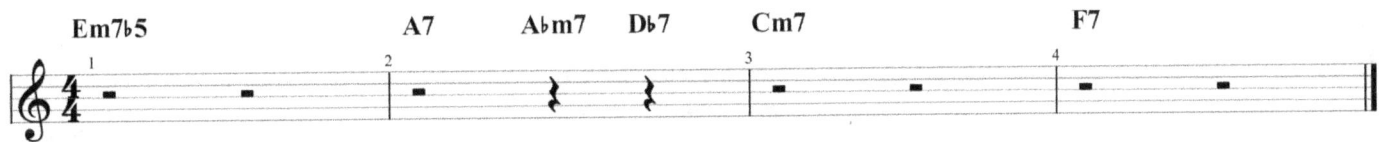

We will begin by voice leading the above progression on the top four strings of the guitar. Watch out for any alterations I add to the chords to smooth out the path of each voice.

Example 5k:

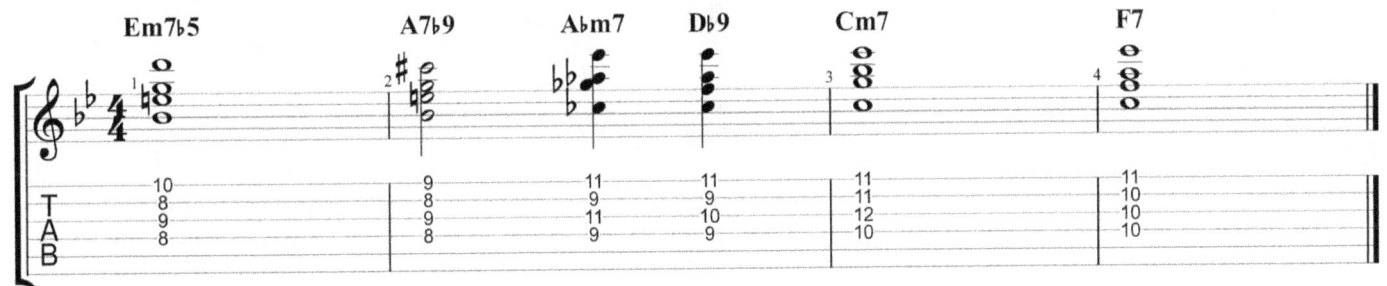

Example 5l:

Explore as many starting points and permutations as you can before experimenting with voicings on the middle four strings. The following ideas will get you started:

Example 5m:

Example 5n:

As your confidence develops, try applying these ideas to drop 3 voicings with a bass note on the fifth string.

Em7b5 (Drop 3)

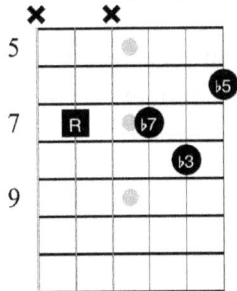

Work through different tunes looking for opportunities to use secondary dominants, tritone substitutions and their ii chords, and apply these techniques to different keys.

The following chart summarises the steps that can be taken to add a tritone substitution to a secondary dominant chord using the chord sequence Cm7 – F7. Make sure you understand each step in the process.

S.D. = Secondary Dominant

T.T. = Tritone Substitution

When you add tensions to the tritone substitution, stick to using 9s, #11s and 13s, although as your skills progress you may wish to experiment more.

Chapter Six: Voice Leading with Substitutions

In this chapter, I want to introduce you to two important substitutions that occur regularly in jazz, and when combined with secondary dominant and tritone ideas, allow us to build exciting new chord sequences from 'standard' progressions.

As you are reading this book, you may well already be aware of the first substitution.

You can play a m7 chord on the 3rd of a Maj7 chord to form a Maj9 chord.

Even though this is a common substitution, we will look at an application you may not have come across.

Let's take a look at an example using a CMaj7 chord.

The 3rd of CMaj7 is E, so the rule tells us that we can play an Em7 chord instead of the CMaj7 to create a CMaj9 sound. Let's check out the notes of CMaj7 and Em7 to see how this works.

Interval from C	1	3	5	7	9
CMaj7	C	E	G	B	
Em7		E	G	B	D

As you can see, the notes in Em7 are the same as the notes of a rootless CMaj9 chord, so any CMaj7 chord can be replaced by an Em7 chord.

Here are some useful voicings you can use to play this substitution. The root note of C is marked in grey for reference only. The root note of the Em7 is the 3rd CMaj7.

There are many more, so go through the process of finding a CMaj7 voicing and raising the root up by a tone to form an Em7 / CMaj9 in as many positions as you can.

As we saw previously, it is important to learn to see substitutions as a series of intervals built around a root note. Make sure you are always able to immediately find the R, 3, 5, 7 and 9 of any chord. One of your practice goals should be to develop instant interval recognition around any root note.

The second substitution we will look at is a little less obvious and doesn't follow any 'rules' as such. However, it is an extremely common idea in jazz:

Any m7 chord can be replaced by a 7 or a 7(#9) chord.

In a iim7 – V7 progression, this substitution is similar to playing the secondary dominant of the V chord.

In the above example, C7 is the secondary dominant of F7, but it is also a dominant version of the original Cm7 chord. The C7 is played *after* the Cm7, but it could *replace* the Cm7 chord for the whole bar although care must be taken to avoid clashes with the melody notes that were written over the original minor chord.

To help avoid this potential clash, dominant substitutions of minor chords are often played with a added #9 tension. The reason for this can be seen in the following table.

Interval	1	b3 / 3	5	b7	#9
Cm7	C	Eb (D#)	G	Bb	
C7#9	C	E	G	Bb	D# / Eb

As you can see, the #9 of C7#9 (D#/Eb) is the same note as the b3 in Cm7 (Eb).

By adding the #9 to the dominant chord we keep more notes in common with the original m7 chord so it is easier for the original melody to accept the substitution. The melody notes of a song will often include a b3 on a m7 chord. If we substitute this m7 chord for a straight 7 chord we create a clash, but if we substitute the m7 chord for a 7#9 chord, the original b3 / #9 is still heard in the harmony part so the substitution is more forgiving.

Play through the following harmonisations to get a feel for the difference between substituting a m7 chord for a 7 and a 7#9 chord.

Cmaj7   Em7   Am7

Cmaj7   E7   Am7

Cmaj7   E7#9   Am7

Let's combine the two substitutions covered in this chapter into a musical context before moving on to playing these ideas with good voice leading.

We will begin with a ii V I sequence in C and develop it with the substitutions.

Cmaj7   Dm7   G7

The first step is to substitute the CMaj7 in bar two for an Em7, as we saw at the beginning of this chapter.

Cmaj7   Em7   Dm7   G7

Next, let's add secondary dominant chords to both the Em7 and the Dm7 chords:

Cmaj7   B7   Em7   A7   Dm7   G7

Now we can change the Dm7 to a D7#9 (although you may wish to view this as the secondary dominant chord of G7).

Staff 1: | Cmaj7 B7 | Em7 A7 | Dm7 D7#9 | G7 | (4/4)

Finally, to keep the harmonic rhythm moving every two beats, let's add the tritone substitution of G7 in the last bar.

Staff 2: | Cmaj7 B7 | Em7 A7 | Dm7 D7#9 | G7 Db9 | (4/4)

Although we will continue this process further, this is a good point to stop and play some basic chords for the progression so far.

It is important to begin with these 'basic' chords to get a good feel for how the progression sounds before applying voice leading techniques. Compare this sequence with the original ii V I in C Major and you'll see how far it is possible to come once you understand how to use substitutions.

As you become more familiar with this sequence, start to explore voice leading opportunities on different string groups. Don't forget to experiment with extensions and alterations as you get more confident.

Here are just a few ways through the changes.

Example 6a:

Example 6b:

Now let's take a look at another couple of substitution ideas that can be added.

Play through the next examples with basic 'root position' chords before working through the voice leading ideas in each example. It is very important that you learn to hear the root movement of the chord changes before working through the voice leading exercises. If you can, try to record a bassline to help you practice the following examples. A strong bassline will help you to hear how each voicing works in context, especially with voicings that have no root and/or are heavily altered.

I'm not a massive fan of the two 'D' chords in bar three, I think it holds back the harmonic movement of the progression, so I will use a tritone substitution here and replace the D7 with its b5 substitution, Ab. I use a '7#11' chord here as the #11 of Ab is the note D, which becomes the 5th of the G7 in the next chord.

The Ab7#11 will also work well as a 'no root' Ab7b9#11 chord, although I have not used it here as I first want to clearly show you the root movement in the following example. As always, experiment to see which extensions suit your ears. Remember that melody is always a consideration when choosing substitutions.

Cmaj7   B7   Em7   A7   Dm7   Ab7#11   G7   Db9

Example 6c:

Cmaj7   B7   Em7   A7b9   Dm7   Ab7#11   G7   Db9   Cmaj7

Now I'm going to substitute the Em7 for an E7#9 as discussed earlier:

Cmaj7   B7   E7#9   A7   Dm7   Ab7#11   G7   Db9

Example 6d:

Cmaj7   B7   E7#9   A7   Dm7   Ab7b9#11   G7   Db9   Cmaj7

Next I can replace the B7 chord with its tritone substitution (F7):

Cmaj7   F9   E7#9   A7   Dm7   Ab7#11   G7   Db9

Example 6e:

Cmaj7	F9	E7#9	A7	Dm7	Ab7b9#11	G9	Db9	Cmaj7

```
      1                 2                   3                   4                           5
T   7      5          3      5          5       5          5       4                    3
A   5      4          5      5          3       3          3       4                    3
B   5      5          5      7          5       5          4       4                    2
    5      5          6      5          3       4          3       3                    2
```

To create a chromatically descending bassline I can also replace the A7 in bar two with its tritone substitution, Eb7:

Cmaj7	F9	E7#9	Eb9	Dm7	Ab7#11	G7	Db9

```
      1              2              3              4
```

Example 6f:

Cmaj7	F9	E7	Eb9	Dm9	Ab7b9#11	G9	Db9	Cmaj9

```
      1                 2                  3                   4                          5
T  12      10         12     11         10      11         10      9                    8
A   9       8          9     10          9       7         10      8                    7
B  10      10         12     11         10      10          9      9                    9
   10      10         11     10          8       9         10      8                    7
```

The previous few examples show how you can use step-by-step substitutions to go from something as simple as…

Cmaj7				Dm7		G7	

```
      1              2              3              4
```

…to something as interesting as:

Cmaj7   F9   E7#9   Eb9   Dm7   Ab7#11   G7   Db9

The important thing, however, is to use good voice leading when you play through the changes otherwise the ideas can sound disjointed and awkward. It is normally perfectly acceptable to adjust extensions and alterations on any voicing to smooth the transition between each chord change.

Remember too that many things depend on context, such as what band or line-up are you playing in. You may not have as much flexibility to use these type of substitutions when you're working as a vocal duo. Often singers need to hear a root note in the bass of the chord and, unless they are very talented, more 'distant' substitutions may cause a train wreck.

Also, if you start pulling out all these articulate substitution ideas in an unrehearsed situation, you may find that you distract other musicians in the band. Remember that substitutions can often take you away from the original harmony of the piece so sometimes discussion and rehearsal are the best ways to go.

One thing I'm always quick to point out to students is that 'theoretically possible' and 'musically appropriate' are not synonymous!

So why then, am I asking you to work through these substitutions?

Well, there are three reasons. Firstly, with a well-rehearsed band and good rhythmic placement, substitution ideas can sound jaw-droppingly wonderful. Listen to the great chord melody improvisers such as Joe Pass, Jim Hall, Wes Montgomery, Kurt Rosenwinkel, Lenny Breau, Barney Kessel and, of course, the sublime Ted Greene, to hear all of these ideas in action.

Sometimes all it takes is just one subtle substitution to make the audience sit up and take notice.

The second reason for working through these substitutions is simple: practice! Throughout this book I have stressed the importance of seeing each voicing as a series of intervals and not simply a chord shape. By practicing substitutions in this way you get to immerse yourself in many different chord types which can be played all over the neck. Also, as these substitutions can be applied to any chord sequence, there are many chord permutations that can be used.

As you work through more and more substitutions on different tunes, your interval and chord recognition will improve dramatically, as will the speed at which you can improvise with interesting substitutions.

The third main reason to work on these substitutions is to teach you to reharmonise jazz standards and build a path into chord melody. Using substitutions is a productive way to find your own voice when playing tunes that have been heard for over fifty years.

Another important use of substitutions is to allow us to access melody notes that lie outside the expected harmony of the chord.

For example, take a look at the following melody:

The note Eb (D#) lies outside the diatonic scale in the key of C Major, so how could we harmonise this note?

One way would be to use the secondary dominant chord of C Major, G7. The melody note forms a b13/#5 from the root note G, so G7#5 is a reasonable choice:

The note D#/Eb is the 9th in the tritone substitution of G7 (Db), so Db9 is also a good choice:

We can also add the iim7 chord before the Db9:

It's also possible to combine the original G7#5 substitution back into the above sequence.

A good knowledge of substitutions can help us to find creative harmonisations for any unexpected melody note.

The goal is to become as comfortable with common substitution ideas as possible by developing a practice approach that allows you to incorporate substitutions. This will greatly improve your freedom and reflexes on the guitar.

Chapter Seven: More Substitution Exercises

We saw in Chapter Four how to add secondary dominant chords to a harmonised scale of C Major, let's now extend that exercise to incorporate tritone substitutions and their ii chords.

We will stay in the key of C for simplicity although you should do this exercise in all common keys. First, refresh your memory of the harmonised scale of C Major:

As before, we will precede each chord with its secondary dominant:

However, this time instead of playing each secondary dominant, play the *tritone substitution* of each secondary dominant. Begin by playing each substitution as a 'normal' dominant 7th to hear the characteristic sound of this substitution.

Example 7a:

Once again, the visual nature of the guitar is our enemy here, as it is all too easy to simply play a dominant 7 chord a semitone above the root of the following chord. It is very important that you learn *not* to rely on this method. Each time, go through the mental process of finding the secondary dominant and then substituting it for its tritone.

My mental process sounds like this:

"The dominant of D is A, the b5 of A is Eb" etc.

Don't take a shortcut here, it will make life harder in the long run.

Play through the new sequence in each of the ways discussed in Chapter Three. Keep the melody note ascending or descending and take the time to play through this sequence in limited fret ranges of the guitar. Example 6h shows one way to play through these changes in a limited range on the top four strings.

Example 7b:

Next, to help smooth the voice leading, play every tritone substitution as a 7b9 chord by replacing the root with a b9.

Example 7c:

Create your own variations of the previous two exercises. For example, you could play every diatonic chord as a 9th by raising the root a tone, or you could add a specific extension/alteration to every tritone dominant.

As your abilities improve, create a logical approach to combining these extensions and alterations on every chord. It can help to draw a table to organise your practice time. One example that explores introducing 9ths could be as follows:

Played each diatonic chord as a:	Play each tritone substitution as a:
7th	7
7th	b9
7th	9
9th	7
9th	9
9th	b9
9th	Alternate 9 and b9

You could then begin to introduce b5s or #5s to each tritone substitution, or 13ths to both the diatonic chords and the tritone substitutions.

Before you launch into these exercises, make sure you can voice basic 7th chords in multiple limited-fret areas on the guitar while exploring different voicings and string groups. Don't worry too much about rhythm when you first begin these exercises – the priority is always voice leading and interval recognition.

Let's reintroduce the iim7 chord of each tritone substitution. Remember, it is essential to be able to 'think' your way through each change, which becomes more difficult as we add more substitutions.

First play the ii V tritone substitution sequence with root position chords:

Example 7d:

Again, you may wish to smooth out the voice leading by using dominant 9 chords instead of the dominant 7ths on the tritone substitutions, just as we did in example 5i.

Next, arrange these chords with tight voice leading on four-string groups. Here is one route through the changes on the middle four strings with R-7 chords:

Example 7e:

Work through the above sequence in different areas of the guitar using four-string groups before adding the extension and alterations suggested in the table above.

Finally, let's rework the previous example to include extensions and alterations so that we may smooth the voice leading even further.

Example 7f:

Take time to consider why each extension or alteration has been used, and find as many ways around this progression as you can. Take an organised approach to adding extensions and alterations as you saw earlier, although you should always take particular care when adding 13ths to minor chords. Let your ear be the judge.

Notice that I have used both a iim7b5 – V, and a iim7 – V when resolving to m7 chords in bars one to three. These choices worked for my ears, but you may have a different opinion. Explore these ideas as much as you can, but remember that the real-world decision will always come down to what notes are in the melody.

Spend as much time as you can working in limited fretboard regions and always consider which intervals are available on each chord, where to play them, and the voice leading they provide between each successive chords.

Further Practice Ideas

The following ideas will help you to expand your exploration of voice leading with secondary dominants, tritone substitutions, and their iim7 chords. This list is by no means exhaustive and will take many diligent months of practice to work through.

- Repeat the diatonic scale exercises in this book in all common jazz keys: Bb, Eb, C, G and F.

- *Descend* through the harmonised Major scale using a) secondary dominants, b) tritone substitutions, c) ii chords preceding both a and b.

- Repeat all of the exercises in this book using the harmonised Harmonic Minor scale.

- Repeat all the exercises using the harmonised Melodic Minor scale.

- Add secondary dominant chords to chromatically ascending/descending key centres. For example, Eb7 – E7 – F7 or Eb7 – Em7 – Fm7. Keep the voice leading as close as possible.

The most important thing you can do with these ideas is to apply them to real tunes. Rehearse them with your band and try out as many ideas as possible. If you don't have a band, try recording a bassline or use a looper pedal so you can always hear a strong, regular bassline when you try out substitutions with close voice leading. If you can record or loop more than one track, try playing both the bassline and the melody so you can hear the real musical effect of a substitution decision you make.

While you're practicing, keep in mind that alterations, extensions and substitutions should be introduced to smooth the voice leading between successive chords. If there is a tone movement between one chord and the next, try to find a substitution or alteration that allows you to make this movement into a semitone or remove it altogether.

We have covered many theoretical concepts in the previous few chapters, but the only rule is that the melody always comes first. Even if you feel that something is 'technically' correct, if it makes the melody sound bad, don't use it.

Chapter Eight: Application

In this chapter, we will consolidate many of the techniques shown in this book and apply them to part of a new tune, *Some of The Things You Are*. This song's harmony is based on the chord changes to *All The Things You Are*.

The chords in the first eight bars of this tune are:

These few bars are rife with substitution opportunities, but first let's take a look at a few ways to play this sequence on the guitar.

Example 8a:

Example 8b:

Now let's add some extensions and alterations to help the voice leading flow smoothly.

Example 8c:

Fm9   B♭m7   E♭7#5♭9   A♭maj9   D♭maj9   G7#5♭9   C6/9   Cmaj7

Example 8d:

Fm7   B♭m9   E♭13   A♭maj7   D♭maj7   G7♭9   Cmaj7   C6/9

Of course, there are many ways to voice these chords and by now you know how to explore these options. Refer back to Chapter Three if you need more ways to practice these progressions. Keep looking for the closest ways to voice these chords and experiment with different tensions on the dominant chords. The above examples barely scratch the surface.

Let's ignore melody for now and look at some possible substitutions that could be used over this chord sequence.

We will begin by adding secondary dominant chords where there is not already a V7 – I movement:

I have included the Cm7 chord in bar nine to show the use of the secondary dominant G7#5 in bar eight.

The above sequence could be played with basic voicings in the following way. In most 'static' chords I have used two voicings of the same chord to add some interest.

Example 8e:

Don't worry about voice leading for now, but find a few ways to play this sequence to get a feel for how the secondary dominant chords affect the harmony.

Next, let's add some tritone substitutions to this progression. We can play b5 (tritone) substitutions on either the secondary dominant chords or the original dominant chords (Eb7 and G7).

Remember that a true tritone substitution is only when a *dominant* chord is replaced with another *dominant* chord a b5 distance away.

Study bar one. We can use a tritone substitution to replace the (dominant) F7#9, but we wouldn't normally be able to use one if the chord was a Fm7 as it not a dominant 7 chord.

With these substitutions we could turn the above sequence into:

These chords can be played as basic root position voicings as follows:

Example 8f:

| Fm7 | B13 | Bbm7 | E7 | Eb7 | A7#5 | Abmaj7 | D9 |

| Dbmaj7 | Ab7 | G7 | Db13 | Cmaj7 | G7#5 |

The next stage is to add some ii chords. Remember, these chords can be the ii of the original chord, or they can be the ii of the tritone substitution.

These substitutions can also be played *in addition to* or *instead of* the original V chord.

| Fm7 | F#m9 | B13 | Bbm7 | E7 | Eb7 | Em7 | A7 | Abmaj7 | Am7 | D9 |

| Dbmaj7 | Ebm9 | Ab13 | G7 | Abm7 | Cmaj7 | Ab7#5 | D9 | Db7#9 |

I have 'borrowed' two beats of bar seven to approach the D9 with its tritone substitution (Ab) to create a turnaround into the Cm7 in bar 9.

Play through the sequence in the following way and also find new ways to voice these chords.

Example 8g:

The previous example shows just one way to use substitutions on these changes although it is, of course, possible to combine secondary dominants without tritones and ii chords with the previous ideas.

For example, the first few bars of this sequence could be played in the following way using a 'mix and match' approach. The tritone substitution is used in bar one, and a simple secondary dominant is used in bar two. (Bb7b9 works well here).

You can learn by simple trial and error. Trust your ears to find your favourite musical choices.

Now let's arrange example 8g with good voice leading on four strings. In the following examples I have used extensions and alterations at will to smooth the voice leading.

One possible way to voice this progression is shown below:

Example 8h:

Find other routes around this sequence using good voicing leading on other string groups and in other regions of the guitar.

An essential consideration for each substitution is always the melody of the tune in each bar. As your reharmonisation skills improve, you will learn to quickly account for melody notes when you substitute chords, although for now it is probably more useful to go through the step by step process I have shown in this book and then look for clashes that you may need to adjust.

Get a Real Book and check out the melody for All the Things You Are. In particular, pay attention to the melody in bar 4. If we were playing the melody to All the Things You Are over the changes written in the previous example, the G in bar four might form an 'interesting' tension over the D9. It could be worth playing a D9sus4 or D11 chord at this point to avoid the clash, but experiment to see what you prefer.

Always be aware of the melody note and what interval it forms against any substitutions you use. As you practice, you'll naturally start to combine substitution ideas with good voice leading. These chord ideas, coupled with a strong awareness of melody will make your jazz rhythm guitar parts well rounded, interesting and musical.

The key to building proficiency at voice leading is experimentation and logical study. Refer back to the voicing ideas in Chapter Three to help you organise your practice and to introduce intervals you may not have previously considered.

Conclusions and Further Study

The concepts in this book are quite advanced and go way beyond the normal chord repertoire of the average gigging guitarist. However, these techniques are commonplace in jazz and more modern classical music. Each substitution idea allows us to access interesting and exciting harmonies while the essential and fundamental aspect of voice leading enables the creation of smooth, fluid rhythm guitar parts.

The ideas behind this book are summarised as follows:

- Practice moving as few notes as possible between chords.

- Use extensions and alterations to eliminate or reduce voice movement

- Any chord can be approached by a secondary dominant

- Tritone substitutions can be used on functional dominants, including secondary dominant.

- Tritone substitutions and secondary dominants can be approached by their ii chord

- Melody is king! Adjust substitutions to avoid clashes with the written melody

While the use of chord voicings and substitutions can depend on the playing situation (are you in a vocal duo? Is there a bass? What is the piano playing?) working on voice leading in the practice room should be a top priority. Practicing voice leading and limiting the note movements between each successive chord quickly helps us to see the guitar neck in terms of intervals. The confidence that comes with this vision cannot be understated. While the initial practice of interval recognition is difficult and time-consuming, the benefit to our playing and music is almost indescribable.

Before too long we can begin to improvise with harmony, selecting chord qualities and textures in the same way a painter selects a colour from a palette. When we instantly see the neck in terms of intervals organised around a root note, the richness of every possible colour becomes available.

This level of vision and ability does take a lot of work, and it will become a lifetime's study, but the potential results will set you apart from every other guitarist.

To practice the voicing ideas in this book simply apply them to your favourite jazz standards and be exhaustive in your studies. Get *inside* the song's structure and you will find chord relationships you didn't know existed.

To organise your practice, begin from one of the four inversions of a particular chord structure (drop 2, drop 3, etc.), and play through the sequence using the closest possible R-7 voicings. Next introduce simple extensions and alterations to explore whether a note can be held over from one chord to the next. Aim to move only one or two notes between chords.

Use tritone substitutions on the existing functional dominant chords and then see how adding their ii chords affects the voice leading. Next, logically work through other substitution options beginning with secondary dominants to see how these affect the harmony before once again seeing if it is appropriate to add their ii chords.

Remember m7 chords can often be substituted for 7#9 chords, which then allows for further tritone substitution.

Finally, do a melody check to see whether your new chord sequence works with the original tune of the song. If it doesn't fit the melody, make the necessary adjustments.

As your voice leading and reharmonisation skills improve, you will naturally begin to take a 'melody first' approach, choosing each extension, alteration and substitution to directly compliment and enhance the melody.

This level of awareness does take a while to develop so I suggest you work through the steps above to become comfortable with the basic techniques and allow your melodic awareness to develop naturally in parallel. It helps tremendously if you know the tune of the song inside out, so make sure you can play the melody from memory in a few different locations on the guitar.

To help you lay out the song on the guitar neck, it is often useful to play a 'melody and bass' version of the song. Play the bassline on the bottom two strings of the guitar and voice the melody on the higher strings. There may be a few stretches, but doing this really helps to internalise the structure of the song and prevents you from getting lost. You'll also always know what the melody note is over each chord.

This book is the starting point of a fun, rewarding and lifelong study of voicings and harmonisation on the guitar. It will greatly enhance your musical ability and understanding of the instrument.

Good luck and have fun!

Joseph

Other Books from Fundamental Changes